Totem Poles

TOTEM POLES

Pat Kramer

VANCOUVER · VICTORIA · CALGARY

Totem poles come from the creative expression of people

Acknowledgements

Sincere thanks are due to the many native people across British Columbia who helped to give this book its shape. Many took time to give directions and make suggestions. Others kindly shared their traditions and ceremonies. Still others prepared many a barbecue salmon feast. To the native dancers, artists, carvers, friends and passers-by who allowed me to photograph them, and to those who for one reason or another do not appear here, an expression of appreciation. To those of my adult students at the Native Education Centre who acted as my inspiration; to all those who gave me permission to intrude with my camera; to those gracious elders who were kind, (though my time has been all too short); to my native friends who smiled and gently corrected me; and to my native grandfather who took me travelling at an early age, I express my gratitude. A sampling of these fine people and their children appears on the page opposite.

From these fine folks I bring a message. When asked what they would most like to see in contemporary writings, many wish to send one clear

To the two little Coast Salish girls whose photo appears here but whose guardians thought should remain unnamed, here is the fulfillment of a promise. One fine summer afternoon at the War Canoe Races, these two sparkling youngsters heard I was doing a book about totem poles. After circling around a bit, they shyly implied that they might like to appear in this book. "But you are not totem poles!" my adult wit gently teased them. "Oh yes, we make a very fine totem pole," they insisted. So here you are. I have kept my word. Now the book is complete and no finer totem pole can be found within these pages. For the best "totem" of all is the creative enthusiasm of a new generation.

message. First People are not trapped in the past; they are not living in 1750 or 1850 or 1950. And though they have endured great hardship, they did not perish. Today, they are alive and well. It is true they are part of an animated tradition with strong roots in the past. However, tradition is not static. Those of the present are reshaping their lives (as they always have) for the benefit of future generations. While respecting the past, the present generation carries on, always adapting, always innovating, always improving their ways. This is the way all vibrant societies thrive.

Message received, and message delivered.

There are others to whom we owe recognition but whose names are not recorded. Spiraling back in time are countless but nameless master carvers and their apprentices who inspired the carvers of the present. Though their names may be obscured with the passing of the seasons, their work breathes through their successors to the present moment.

Heritage House Publishing Company Ltd.
#108 – 17665 66A Avenue
Surrey, BC V3S 2A7
www.heritagehouse.ca

Library and Archives Canada Cataloguing in Publication

Kramer, Pat
  Totem poles / Pat Kramer.

Includes bibliographical references and index.
ISBN 978-1-894974-44-8

  1. Totem poles—British Columbia—History. 2. Indians of North America—Material culture—British Columbia. 3. Indian wood-carving—British Columbia. 4. Indians of North America—British Columbia—Antiquities. 5. British Columbia—Antiquities. I. Title.

E78.B9K72 2008   971.1'100497   C2008-902184-3

Originally published by Altitude Publishing
Edited by Anne Norman
Design by Stephen Hutchings and Sandra Davis
Maps by Sandra Davis

Printed in Canada

  This book was printed using vegetable-based inks on chlorine-free paper that was harvested using responsible forest practices.

Heritage House acknowledges the financial support for its publishing program from the Government of Canada through the Canada Book Fund (CBF), Canada Council for the Arts, and the province of British Columbia through the British Columbia Arts Council and the Book Publishing Tax Credit.

Although extreme care has been taken to ensure that all information presented in this book is accurate and up-to-date, neither the author nor the publisher can be held responsible for any errors.

Contents

Totem Poles is organized according to the following colour scheme:

The Origin and History of Totem Poles ....

Totem Pole Symbols and Ceremonies ....

Identifying Totem Figures ....

Land of the Totem Poles ....

Recommended Reading and Index..................

1. The Origin and History of Totem Poles

Skidegate in Haida Gwaii in 1878 was a thriving village at the apex of the Golden Age of totem poles. Dr. George M. Dawson, the photographer, and James Deans, a contemporary researcher, note that Haida clan status was partially indicated by the height of one's pole. All poles shown here were taken down at the behest of missionaries about a decade later.

Long, long ago, obscured by the passage of time, people living along the Pacific Coast of North America developed a culture based on the abundance surrounding them. Tidal pools yielded hoards of shellfish. Rivers were laden with migrating salmon. The air was filled with flocks of waterfowl. Forests soared with mighty trees. To survive and thrive in this environment, nameless individuals painstakingly invented tools, refined their techniques, and passed on their knowledge. In turn, their expertise in the technology of survival freed up the leisure time required to establish a rich and vibrant cultural life. Long-ago artisans turned to the decorative potential of stone and wood, particularly cedar. Excavated tools suggest that coastal people were working with wood by about 5000 BC. The embodiment of eons of artistic traditions can be seen today, woven into the fascinating aboriginal art and totem poles of the First Nations of the region known as the Northwest Coast.

Early Art and Objects

Anthropologists estimate that cultural patterns based on wealth and leisure time permit certain individuals to specialize at least part-time in the arts. Along the Northwest Coast, these patterns were well established by 3500 BC. Because wooden objects disintegrate over time, stone carvings and various tools are the only

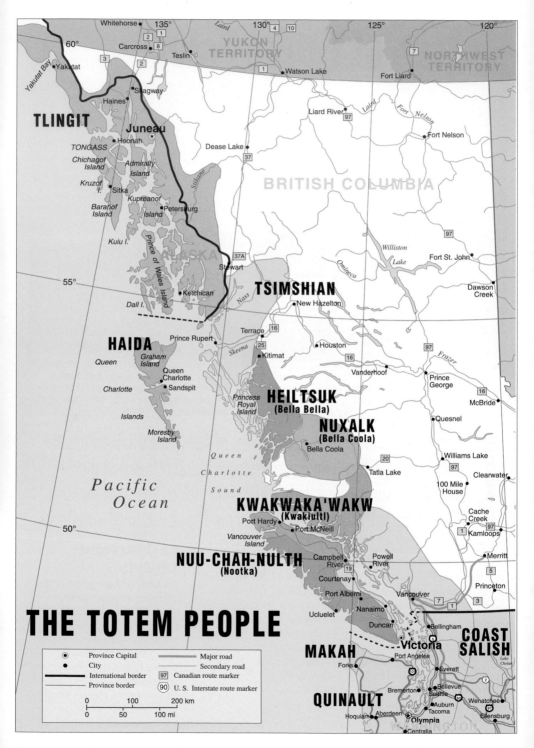

THE TOTEM PEOPLE

TLINGIT

TONGASS
Chichagof Island
Admiralty Island
Kruzof I.
Sitka
Baranof Island
Kupreanof Island
Kuiu I.
Prince of Wales Island
Dall I.

Juneau ☆
Hoonah
Petersburg
Ketchican

HAIDA

Queen
Graham Island
Queen Charlotte
Sandspit
Charlotte
Islands
Moresby Island

Whitehorse • 135° 130° [4] [10] 125° 120°
[2] [1]
Carcross • [8]
60°
[3] Teslin •
[2]
Laird
YUKON TERRITORY
Watson Lake
[1] • Watson Lake
NORTHWEST TERRITORY
[7]
Fort Liard •

Yakutat Bay
• Yakutat
Skagway •
Haines •

Liard River •
[97]
Laird
Fort Nelson
• Fort Nelson

ALASKA
Dease Lake •
[37]
BRITISH COLUMBIA
Williston Lake
Omineca
Fort St. John •

55°
Stewart
[37A]
Nass
TSIMSHIAN
• New Hazelton
Skeena
Terrace [16]
[25]
• Kitimat
• Houston
[16]
• Vanderhoof

Dawson Creek •

Prince Rupert •
Frazer
[97]
Prince George
[16]
• McBride

HEILTSUK
(Bella Bella)
Princess Royal Island

NUXALK
(Bella Coola)
Bella Coola

• Quesnel

Queen
Charlotte
Sound

Pacific Ocean

• Williams Lake
[97]
Clearwater •
Tatla Lake
[20]
100 Mile House
Cache Creek
KWAKWAKA'WAKW
(Kwakiutl)
Port Hardy •
Port McNeill •
Vancouver Island
[1]
Kamloops

50°
NUU-CHAH-NULTH
(Nootka)
Campbell River
[19]
Courtenay •
Port Alberni •
Powell River
Vancouver •
Merritt •
[5]
Princeton •
[7] [1]
[3]

Ucluelet •
Nanaimo •
Duncan •
Bellingham •
Victoria ⊚
COAST SALISH
Lake Chelan

MAKAH
Port Angeles •
Forks •
Everett •
[2]

QUINAULT
Hoquiam •
Aberdeen •
Bremerton •
Seattle
Bellevue •
Wenatchee •
Auburn •
Tacoma
Olympia ⊚
Centralia •
Ellensburg •
WASHINGTON

Legend

⊙	Province Capital	Major road
•	City	Secondary road
	International border	[97] Canadian route marker
	Province border	⑨⓪ U. S. Interstate route marker

0   100   200 km
0   50   100 mi

The art of Northwest Coast Natives is eons old. Only the medium has changed over the centuries. This modern totem figure, said to be the first man to discover the earth, is hauntingly similar to an ancient petroglyph located deep in the forest near Bella Coola, BC.

jects; bone implements; chisels; sharp blades of nephrite; and well-decorated baskets, canoe paddles, and wooden storage boxes.

Other community sites excavated along the coast of present-day British Columbia, dating from AD 500 to 1200, have revealed carved combs, crafted charms and amulets, rounded human-figure stone bowls, and bone pins decorated with animal and human heads. All these objects show proficient stone and woodworking skills. Even a paint pallet was recovered. Though no totem poles or wooden totem figures are known from this period, small decorative objects in everyday use show a highly developed symbol system. The figure of Wolf shows up in one beautifully carved comb (ca. AD 800), as does Raven (ca. 1000 BC) and a number of unidentified large-eyed creatures (ca AD 1000). Though our curiosity is great, researchers can only guess broadly what these creatures meant in their own time.

Rock Art Sites

Over 600 rock art sites are presently known along the Northwest Coast from southwestern Alaska through British Columbia to the lower Columbia River and extending into California. The sites are thought to date from 4500 BC to about AD 1800.

Researchers continue to explore the shapes found in these once-hidden areas and many surmise that they were the work of shamans and their initiates. Young people were introduced to the spiritual side of life through a process of

objects that remain to suggest these patterns. At one site dated to about 1000 BC, researchers uncovered a number of small art objects in everyday use. Another site, dated to 500 BC, yielded copper bracelets, decorated warrior weapons, slate and bone amulets, stone labrets (for pierced lips), sea otter teeth made into mosaics, and handles on chisels decorated with human faces. One rare site, completely underwater, fortuitously preserved ancient wooden and organic objects in an anaerobic environment. Dated to about AD 500, this rich find suggests that the potlatch tradition was well underway and the status of upperclass families already symbolized by heraldic crests. Recovered objects include mauls; antler wedges; small art ob-

Though this photograph was taken in the early 1900s, it shows old-style mortuary figures of the type reported by the first trading ships mapping the coast. These types of carvings predate contact.

vision questing. Sequestered deep within the forest, the fasting initiates first found their "song"—two or three sentences with deep meaning. Eventually, they spoke with animals who changed their lives. The art found along cliffs and ocean shorelines may be either laborious attempts to contact a spirit-animal or a permanent record of the encounter after it occurred.

Rock art sites are decorated with red ochre paintings and known as pictographs, or they are abraded with sharp tools and known as petroglyphs. Though the curvilinear styles are recognizable and the creatures seem linked by some type of mythological framework, researchers can only guess at their exact meaning.

The art forms now seen in the totem poles of coastal Native people extend back over the centuries. Shapes have evolved and slowly varied, but the concept of dividing flat spaces with incised lines and characteristic curved shapes was widely practised from the dawn of civilization. The art of today has never deviated from the roots that make it recognizable as an art form belonging entirely to the First People of the Northwest Coast.

Life before Contact

By AD 1000 and up to the point of contact with Europeans around 1740, Northwest Coast artifacts show that Winter Dance mask ceremonies were a well-established part of life. Various bands of people lived in villages of plank longhouses during the winter, then spread out in summer to work in berry-picking grounds or to

fish in fertile salmon migration areas. Climatic conditions were fairly stable.

At this time, bands developed a workable three-tiered class system. The upper classes lived a privileged life with the obligation to accumulate wealth and then give it all away in an elaborate ceremony known as a potlatch. The middle classes were artisans, cooks, hunters, gatherers, and workers who could rate extra privileges if their artistic works were particularly admired. The underclass were slaves, captured during raids against neighbouring bands. Their very lives depended on the whim of their upper-class owners.

The objects recovered from this period are highly decorated and show that talented members of the band were

John Webber, the artist on Captain Cook's third expedition, drew this rendering of a Nootka longhouse in 1778. This is the first time an academic outsider provided visual evidence of carved or painted poles.

employed full-time to render ceremonial art. Women and men spun and wove mountain goat fleece into blankets. Other pieces of clothing were woven from cedar bark. Watertight bentwood boxes were used for cooking and storage. A shaman's "crown" was made of grizzly bear claws. Chiefs wore carved headdresses with ermine tails. Food dishes were carved into representational shapes. Chiefs owned decorated canes known as talking sticks.

Between 1500 and 1700, several coastal bands incised designs on the interior posts of their large post-and-beam plankhouses. Because of the nature of their nephrite and obsidian tool blades, however, most carved objects were relatively small. The Haida report that special "logs" washed up on their shores during this period and from these they recovered iron. At first contact, several coastal bands already fashioned iron tools. Researchers surmise that these "logs" were masts that floated in from far-away shipwrecks.

It takes strong, durable tools to carve large wooden objects with speed and efficiency. With the few iron tools they owned, long before the arrival of Europeans, some bands were already carving freestanding human-sized wooden mortuary (memorial) figures. The ancient practice of carving of human-sized wooden or stone figures is a characteristic that Northwest Coast Natives share with both the aboriginals of Hawaii and the Maoris of New Zealand, although no academic studies link these peoples or their traditions.

Illustrating the class system, a box held aloft by obedient slaves once contained the remains of an upper-class person.

Sporadic First Russian Contacts: 1740 to 1780

Around 1738, Russian ships and traders arrived along the Northwest Coast and began an active industry in sea otter pelts. In 1741, Captain Vitus Bering landed for six hours at Cape St. Elias, Alaska. He observed carved interior house posts. Whether these carvings resembled modern totem poles is not known. At that time, any totemic or family crest activity was the privilege of the upper classes and therefore would be considered a secret and private matter.

The Sea Otter Trade: 1774 to 1830

Many Europeans visited the region to take advantage of the sea otter trade. In 1774, explorer Juan Pérez of Spain sailed along the coast as far north as Haida Gwaii (the Queen Charlotte Islands) but the weather kept him from landing. Later, Spanish mariners traded in sea otter pelts and enjoyed a lively commerce in copper. As copper was an important component in potlatches, additional Spanish supplies were welcomed.

About 1778, the British began a succession of voyages along the coast. A scientific expedition under the direction of Captain James Cook rested for repairs for three weeks at Nootka Sound on present-day Vancouver Island. Their careful records mention monstrous masks, wooden chests, and ceremonial objects decorated in an elaborate style. They also report carved and painted interior house posts and painted house fronts, but there is no mention of freestanding totem poles. John Webber, the ship's artist on Cook's third and final voyage, painted several renditions of Nootka longhouses. One illustration (page 15) depicts some sort of faces on two interior house posts. His 1778 drawing is the earliest known academic documentation of decorated poles.

An elder holds a talking stick while a totem carver "cleanses" the group with a cedar bough. Talking sticks dated to AD 1000 have been recovered.

The Concept of Transformation

THE CHANGING OF animals and supernatural creatures into other forms or humans, as well as the occasional transformation of humans into animals, is an important component of totem pole stories. Transformation is accomplished without effort and is sometimes referred to as shape shifting. Characterized as "taking off" or "putting on" a skin coat, transformation can be accomplished without a trace of the former creature in evidence.

While in its altered form, the transformed creature may seduce another, win a combat, receive gifts or food, or effect a revenge. Some creatures transform in order to attend human dance ceremonies or to hold their own; a few do it to look in on or assist humans. Trickster figures like Raven are particularly adept at changeovers and in addition to becoming living incarnations, they can manifest as wooden dishes, dirt, pine needles, or totem poles. On Northwest Coast totem poles, transforming figures are carved with large horizontal lips, animal or partially human heads, and partially human bodies. Characteristically, the back, human-shaped legs remain in the haunch position of the animal.

Mosquito

By contrast Webber shows Nootka house exteriors of the day as unornamented.

American, British, French, Spanish, and Italian ships all actively plied the waters along North America's Pacific coast during the heyday of the sea otter trade. Though many forays arrived between 1780 and 1830, these naval traders did not always venture into the villages. Many preferred to remain on board, trading from the quiet security of their ships. However, the trade process had an effect on the Native communities. With the sudden increase in wealth and goods, and an abundance of new metal tools, tradition dictated a corresponding need for the upper classes to mount potlatch feasts. Each chief strained to outdo his rivals in terms of grandeur, honours, memorials, remembrances, and ceremonials. Researchers speculate that totem poles, as they are known today, evolved during this period.

In 1786, the La Pérouse expedition visited the Tlingit people at Lituya Bay, Alaska. Though they travelled with an artist, there is no mention of totem poles. In 1787 Captain George Dixon visited the Native people at Yakutat Bay, Alaska, and Haida Gwaii, BC. Though his artist recorded details of native spoons and trays, there is no mention of totem poles. However, only a few years later, in 1791, Spanish artist José Cardero, a member of the Italian Malaspina expedition, made drawings of several mortuary figures in the same village. Potlatch feasts of the day included the carving and dedication of memorials. This might explain the sudden appearance of the figures.

Tech-niques in handling large logs rapidly improved with the introduction of iron. Native people used new metal parts to fashion tools such as the axe, adze, and curved knife following the form of their earlier implements. Their art forms, story figures, and heraldic crest traditions were already many centuries old and well developed. The new tools were used to produce traditional art forms on a larger scale.

John Jewitt, a sailor captured in 1788, was forced into slavery by the Nootka people. He later escaped, and in 1791 wrote a book—a best-seller in Europe. His writings talk of "great wooden images" on Graham Island and of "large trees carved and painted." John Barlett, artist aboard the *Gustavus* in 1791, made the first rough pen drawing of an outdoor heraldic pole. It is a house support in front of a Haida longhouse. This adds the second academic bit of visual information showing that house front poles were under construction among the Haida people.

Clearly, widespread potlatching activity was afoot. Since iron tools made wood carving simpler and faster and since newfound wealth made necessary the giving of potlatches, the beams of longhouses began to show more decoration both inside and outside, new forms of carvings were produced, and new surnames, new ceremonials, and new crests were sanctified. However, the right to give a potlatch and to own heraldic crests remained firmly in the hands of a few upper-class elders.

Meanwhile, in 1793, Alexander Mackenzie arrived on the Pacific coast. Having made the first overland trek across Canada on foot and by canoe (a decade before the famed Lewis and Clark expedition), his report on inland Natives makes no mention of totem poles among the Bella Coola people. He did however report that some people decorated their interior house posts. Mackenzie was quite surprised by the number of iron pots and tools the Natives owned. In 1792, only one year earlier, along the coast by way of Cape Horn, Captain George Vancouver reported many gigantic wooden human mortuary statues. That same year, Etienne Marchand, leading a French sailing expedition, reported "paintings everywhere, everywhere sculpture, among a nation of hunters." He also reported that "every man is a painter or a sculptor." In 1794, resourceful US Captain Roberts of the *Jefferson* commanded his own carpenters

Argillite is only found on the Haida Gwaii. Made from a soft slate first quarried openly in the 1820s, these small carvings are close in size to traditional arts, and quickly became valued collectibles.

and crew to plane, paint, and erect a freestanding imitation "totem pole" of their own on the tip of Dall Island. Though they erected the structure to aid in their trade negotiations, there is no written report of the Haida's reaction to the first non-native simulated pole. In 1799, American William Sturgis visited the Haida in the vessel *Eliza*. He reported the Haida's love of ornamentation in every aspect of their life, from their personal clothing to elaborately painted designs, inside and outside their longhouses. He makes no mention of interior or exterior totem poles, leading academics to speculate that while tall poles did exist, they were still not common in all the villages.

By 1800, mortuary carvings were being consistently reported, not only in Haida Gwaii, but sporadically for 1500 kilometres (950 miles) up and down the west coast. Furthermore, the carvings seemed to be more numerous and more elaborate with each

passing season. From 1803 to 1805, a Russian expedition under the command of Captains Krusenstern and Liansky packed up a significant collection of Tlingit art and removed it to St. Petersburg. It is not known whether these articles survived later Russian upheavals.

The first documented date known to outsiders involving the formal adoption of totem crests is 1808. A party of inland Gitksan Natives celebrated their recent visit to the new Fort St. James fur-trading post

Collection of Prehistoric Artifacts

THE ROOTS OF totemic figures are found in prehistoric objects recovered from archaeological excavations. A premier collection is on public display weekdays at Simon Fraser University, Museum of Archaeology and Ethnology, Room MPX 8602, Burnaby, BC, V5A 1S6, (604) 291-3325.

The first true freestanding totem poles were apparently constructed by the inland Tsimshian, Gitksan, and Nisga'a peoples along the Nass and Skeena Rivers. Sought after and acquired by museum collectors in the late 1800s, many were shipped around the world. A few were saved, restored, or replicated and stand today in and around Kitwanga, BC.

by adopting crests and building a detached totem pole. That particular totem pole featured representations of European breeds of dogs, the fortified fort, and wide wagon roads. Certainly not the Gitsan's first freestanding pole, scholars disagree on when the people of the Skeena and Nass Rivers started building detached poles. Some guess as early as 1775, though by following the path of iron tools, that date could be some decades later.

In 1820, a black soft stone called argillite was discovered (or revealed to the outside world) at Slatechuck Mountain on Haida Gwaii. With the sea otter trade in rapid decline,

the Haida eagerly began to fashion the material into carved pipes, bowls, and small copies of totem poles. Curio dealers, just beginning to discover the beauty of west coast art, snapped up the items from mariners. As soon as argillite items were put up for sale in 1826, a Finnish trader in the service of a Russian-American company assembled a collection and sent it back to Finland. Sadly, the assemblage was later destroyed in a museum fire.

Though the objects were made strictly for sale to outsiders, argillite subjects are based on ancient traditions and are closer to the size and scale of native art before con-

tact. In 1822, artist Ludovic Choris, who had travelled on a 15-year voyage around the world, published, in Paris, a detailed drawing of an intricate Haida argillite Raven tongue-thrusting pipe. His illustration is significant because it is the first to show the intricacy of design so well developed among the people.

From 1830 to 1840, the land-based Hudson's Bay Company (HBC) founded Fort Simpson and replaced the declining sea otter trade with an expanded market for marten, bear, otter, and beaver. Native settlements tended to move and to spring up near trading areas.

This photo, taken at a 1903 potlatch, shows a tradition with very ancient roots. The potlatch host holds aloft a copper—the symbol of his wealth. He will later break the copper and disperse pieces of it among his equals. This practice all but ceased about 1920.

Golden Age of Totem Poles: 1830 to 1895

A period of prolific totem pole carving took place during the mid- to late-1800s among all Northwest Coast Native people, especially the Haida, Tlingit, Tsimshian, Gitksan, Nisga'a, and Kwakiutl. Each evolved an active industry producing their own types of totem poles. During this productive era, carving techniques improved, new traditions solidified, and the written recording of old legends began in earnest. (The stories told in Chapter 3 of this book originate from this period.)

It is difficult to pinpoint which native cultures contributed most to the art of early totem pole carving, but the Haida certainly hold an honoured place. By 1830, many Haida served as sailors

"Low Man on the Totem Pole"

THIS COMMON expression refers to someone or something with lack of rank or status. With real totem poles, however the opposite is true. The lowest figures are often considered the most important. Since they are at eye-level to observers they are carved with great attention to detail. Figures placed on the bottom 2 metres (6 feet) of totems are carefully carved and greatly detailed. All totem poles are carved by a master carver and a team of apprentices. The helpers do the high up parts and the master carver finishes the low end of the pole. Higher-up figures are more representational and, if anything, slightly less important.

Frog peeks out from a Bear

on ships up and down the coast. Learning the art of scrimshaw (engraving whale's teeth) from seasoned sailors, they immediately applied the techniques to carving argillite and producing silver jewellery. The Haida were teachers too. When in port between Alaska and the state of Washington, they visited nearby Native communities. Each village received the benefit of considerable Haida expertise. In spite of periodic outbreaks of smallpox, the Haida also began many projects on their own islands. Their villages became a marvelous mixture of longhouses and totem poles. Some Alaskan villagers even hired Haida people to carve their first village poles. However, the Tlingit were quick studies and never repeated the exercise.

During this period, the ceremonies surrounding the carving and raising of totem poles were formalized. Before this period, a few select elders controlled the carving of clan symbols. After 1840, new procedures were adopted to enable a wider range of upper-class people (including the nouveau riche) to legally own heraldic crest symbols and story figures. New carvers established traditions and devised methods to formally pass their skills on to younger carvers. The potlatch too became more standardized and its practice spread to interior and southern bands having no former potlatch traditions.

Fort Victoria was established about 1843 and the Beaver clan was founded from members of older clans—mainly the Eagle clans who had traded earlier with the Russians and early European expeditions.The Beaver clans are people who have the right to trade in beaver pelts.

Between 1850 and 1880, several feuds erupted over totem pole practices. Phratries (native kinship divisions) argued over who was entitled to the tallest poles and who had the rights to use certain figures. To show subservience to a more powerful chief, certain clans were forced to chop off their poles; others were made to cut off or deface offending crests. The most bitter feud broke out along the Nass River. There, rights to the tallest totem led to pole chopping and a brutal murder.

The Decline of the Golden Age

Several factors entered into the rapid decline and the eventual hiatus of the newly developed art of large totem pole carving. Though pole building continued defiantly after 1900 in certain areas such as Alert Bay, strong forces acted to stop the practice completely in most other locations.

The scourge of smallpox from 1832 onwards, and particularly in 1862, decimated many bands and struck the Haida hard. The population on Haida Gwaii estimated at 7000 in 1835, dwindled to 800 by 1885. Though vaccine was brought in, only 500 were vaccinated before thousands perished. During the epidemic, only one person survived after contracting the disease.

Haida survivors of the smallpox epidemic huddle shyly at the village of Yan. Many once-thriving villages were gradually abandoned after 1862 because there were too few survivors to carry on.

Ninstints, Yan, and several other well-developed Haida villages were abandoned when there were too few survivors to carry on. Among the Kwakiutl people, from an estimated population of 17,000 people at contact, the lowest level of 2370 people was reached in 1898. Of these, only 637 were males. There were over 900 vacant positions in the upper-class nobility system. The scale of devastation from outbreaks of both smallpox and measles can hardly be imagined.

The second factor leading to the eventual cessation of totem pole building was missionary work that began in earnest by the mid-1800s. Though totem poles served as heraldic crests and story figures and were never worshipped, well-meaning missionaries mistook the poles for pagan symbols. Pole building gradually ceased in areas where missionaries were active, and mysterious or deliberate fires swept away existing poles. In several cases in Alaska and along the BC coast, the Natives themselves, in bursts of zeal, chopped and burned their own poles.

In 1833, there were a number of new poles raised in HBC's Fort Simpson; by 1853, there was no trace of them. In 1876 a Christian missionary, Henry Collison, arrived in Haida Gwaii and reported totem poles in front of every house, were "fraught with meaning to the people themselves." He went on to report that a fellow missionary at Fort Simpson, "has induced them to take them all down and de-

Maori Poles

ACCORDING TO MAORI belief, the rubbing of noses signifies the mixing of breath and reinforces the breath of the world.

In New Zealand, Maori wood sculptures are not called totem poles, but they do serve some of the same purposes. The hardwood posts are the likenesses of ancestors who are not to be forgotten. Traditionally, the posts served as a family tree or a record for one's progeny, and the people decorated posts

The Maori of New Zealand produce poles

inside and outside their meeting houses. They also embellished most of their everyday objects.

Swirling patterns were applied to weapons, boxes, canoes, flutes, tools, and houses. Grotesque posts were designed to frighten away enemies. Called the Vikings of the Sunrise, the Maoris are known to have arrived in New Zealand from Hawaii about 1000 years ago. There are no academic studies linking these ancient rovers to the Northwest Coast of North America, but the parallels are interesting.

A burial ground along the Fraser River, photographed in the 1920s, illustrates burial figures of the type that mariners first reported for 1500 kilometres (950 miles) along the northwest coast in the decades just before and after 1800. The cross is a modern addition.

stroy them." Collison went on to take similar actions. First the poles at Skidegate, then those at Old Masset, were taken down.

In 1870 a visiting, educated European called the Haida, Bella Bella, Tsimshian, and Tlingit "nations of artists," but much of their activity had already ceased or was carried out in secret. About 1880, the practices surrounding totem pole carving ceased completely among the Haida people as they committed en masse to Christianity. Fortunately, small-sized argillite carvings were popular with collectors and were tolerated because they were seen as encouraging "industriousness" among the people.

By about 1902, missionaries had also effectively discouraged the practices around totem pole carving along the Skeena and Nass Rivers. Among the Gitksan, one lone carver named Illameu continued. Ironically, at the same time that totem pole carving ceased everywhere else, it reached an apex among the Kwakiutl and Nootka people.

An old totem pole lies down to rest near a human grave. Almost as soon as Northwest Coast people began making totem poles in quantity, nineteenth century collectors and museum curators began removing them.

23

However, by 1910, carving had virtually ceased among them too, with the exception of the community of Alert Bay and other isolated communities. Perched on small islands between Vancouver Island and the mainland or in isolated coastal inlets, these little villages stubbornly continued with their old traditions.

Canadian law also played an active role in the decline of totem pole carving. In 1880, the federal government passed the first Indian Act. It makes no mention of feast giving or totem pole carving. But in 1884, the government, with the encouragement of several anthropologists and missionaries, added the soon-to-be-infamous amendment section 116. It forbade the massive giving of "gifts," with imprisonment or large fines as a penalty. Although section 116 was aimed specifically at ending the practice of potlatches, it also affected pole carving because great numbers of poles were constructed in anticipation of potlatch ceremonies.

Forbidding the potlatch effectively ended much totem

Which Ones Are the Eyes?

The "eyes" on this totem are more easily distinguished from a distance than up close

ON SOME POLES it is easy to determine the top and bottom of each creature. In other cases, overlapping shapes make it difficult to sort out the beginning of one figure from the ending of another.

Eyes are defined by eyebrows or by eye sockets that are either pinched to a point at both sides or circular and staring ahead.

Eyes are positioned somewhere near mouths. Ovoid shapes, on the other hand, are decorations used to fill spaces. Sometimes the ovoid space filler can be mistaken for an extra eye or a "hidden" creature. Are there extra creatures hidden on totem poles? Generally, there are not.

Illustrated here is Wolf with a long mouth placed vertically. Its eye is surrounded with green. The lower segment is its leg hanging down to its claw. The lower double ovoid is not an additional eye or another creature. Native artists sometimes take an X-ray view of animals and place circular or ovoid designs on joints. In this case the ovoid shows that the shoulder is capable of movement.

An unnamed collector about 1900 strikes a Great White Hunter pose, showing off his acquisition of a rare Chilcotin blanket, a chief's ermine-tail headdress, and a button robe. The removal of native items during the last two decades of the 1800s has been referred to as a collecting rampage.

pole carving. Most bands immediately complied; others ignored the law; a few bands actually increased their holding of potlatches masquerading as "celebrations for the king's coronation" or "Christmas giving to the poor." Many arrests were made. In some cases, plea bargains were arranged. The Native community could sell their regalia and artworks to anthropologists, or their elders could go to jail. In 1885, Bill Uslick of the Pyeachten Reserve at Chilliwack was sentenced to three months in prison for holding a potlatch. Many others were fined in the range of $15—a huge sum at the time. Outsiders consid-

ered the potlatch "wasteful" and harmful to the process of assimilation into white society. Most Native communities complied, but Alert Bay near Vancouver Island remained defiant. Continuing in their old ways, the people of Alert

By the 1840s, the Haida were carving traditional designs into silver jewellry. Though the designs are eons old, some of the crosshatching is adapted from scrimshaw techniques the artists learned when working as mariners aboard sailing ships.

Bay held periodic lavish potlatches. In 1921, Doug Cranmer gave a potlatch so generous that 34 people were charged under section 116. Along with thousands of blankets and food items, he gave away 24 canoes and dozens of sewing machines. Authorities, alarmed at Alert Bay's continuing defiance, came in and seized their extensive potlatch collection of masks and ceremonial objects. Its totem poles were taken soon after. Until 1951, when the law was revoked, potlatches and traditional carving among BC Natives stopped entirely or went underground.

Migration patterns among Native people at this time

also disrupted settled village life and placed additional pressures on long-established customs. In 1887, Alaskan newspapers reported many Natives abandoning their traditional villages for work in salmon-canning factories. While their old villages were left to decay, a few elders proudly erected new poles in front of their houses near the factories. A small renaissance in totem pole building occurred briefly during and after the Klondike Gold Rush of 1897–98. Once again, Native people prospered, and particularly in Alaska and northern British Columbia, there were flurries of potlatches and a number of new poles.

Museum Acquisition Period: 1870 to 1930

While totem pole construction was in decline in certain areas and actively flourishing in others, ethnographers, museum curators, and anthropologists suddenly discovered the art of the Northwest Coast. Particularly for a 20-year period from 1880 to 1900, collectors combed the region in what has been described as a "collecting

The Tradition Continues

THE EARLIEST TYPE of decorated poles mentioned by European traders were interior house posts. Illustrated first in 1778 by John Webber, artist aboard Captain Cook's ship, they served as stage scenery backdrops. All Winter Dances took place in front of house posts. Most depict common story figures and some were outfitted with hidden pulleys or trapdoors so the players or giant wooden puppets could fly or appear and disappear during the ceremonies.

When families moved to their summer quarters, it was common to take their house planks with them, leaving the posts and supporting beams behind. When families returned, the walls were quickly reassembled.

Shown here are a modern Kwakiutl longhouse with its side walls removed and an archival photograph taken about 1910. These two photographs illustrate that today, Native people research museums and archives to rediscover their old designs, and then replicate them as a continuing link in a very old tradition.

Despite a series of interruptions to the tradition, the present-day totem poles in the Kitwancool area of the Skeena River remain true to their origins.

Hawkwoman attends Winter Dance ceremonies

rampage." At times, the researchers almost scrambled over each other. Hundreds of totem poles and hundreds of thousands of objects were removed and found their way to museums in Washington, DC, Chicago, New York, London, Berlin, Paris, New Zealand, Australia, Ottawa, and Montreal—all far from the Pacific northwest coast. Some of the articles were purchased and removed with permission; others were pilfered or extorted. Some of the academic travellers and acquisitors who moved through the area included Marius Barbeau, Franz Boas, George M. Dawson, Wilson Duff, George T. Emmons, Charles Hill-Tout, Captain Ja-

cobsen, Dr. W.H. Kreiger, Charles and William Newcombe, Alex Rasmussen, Edward Sapir, Harlin I. Smith, James G. Swan, John R. Swanton, and Oliver Wells. Captain Jacobsen alone boasted that he acquired 7000 Tlingit items during a single expedition. Berlin museums paid well and often rated first choice. Many of their acquired items disappeared about 1945.

Around 1890, Franz Boas, in particular, made a lasting impression on academic communities. The extensive collection attributed to him was acquired with the considerable help of George Hunt of Fort Rupert, a knowledgeable collector who was half-Tlingit.

Hunt's progeny continue to live and marry among the Kwakiutl people and carve outstanding poles to the present day.

Collectors reached into every community. In 1897, an Anglican clergyman at Masset complained in a letter to the newspaper that "every [native] grave has been rifled and the boxes that contained the bodies left strewn about." By 1910, most traditional objects of value, including many totem poles, had been removed. The Natives had been divested of almost every traditional item they owned.

As early as 1910, tourist ships travelled to Haida Gwaii and curio dealers as well as

museum curators were active in acquiring newly made native goods. Today, some museums disparagingly call these "made for tourist" items, even though at the time this was the only avenue left to traditional Natives to keep their art forms alive.

Today, there is great debate whether these collectors ultimately assisted native cultures by rescuing "evidence" before it was lost or merely accelerated their speedy decline. Much was lost or carelessly handled. In one instance, an Alaskan storekeeper, Mr. Kirberger, gathered totem poles for 25 years. His personal collection was completely destroyed by a fire in 1926. Collections that went to Berlin and St. Petersburg disappeared over the years. Several other collections were lost to museum fires in the 1900s.

The number of traditional items taken by museums expanded beyond reasonable proportions. In 1910, one researcher/collector complained in a letter to his colleague: "There is little in Alaska…I drained the Nass River [area] last year and got all that Willie [Newcombe] left… There is nothing among the Tsimshians…and you have cleaned out the Haidas." Alex Rasmussen, collector of the objects in the Portland Art Museum, declared in 1920 that British Columbia Natives had no objects of value whatsoever left from their former

lives. Most of the objects, he stated, were destroyed, sold, or left behind to decay as the Native people moved into towns. Marius Barbeau, an anthropologist and avid seller of artifacts to museums, reported the same year that there were only 20 poles left intact along the Nass River. Nonetheless, he sold one in 1929 to Sir Henry Thompson. It was

presented as a gift to the French government. Railway officials mistakenly "freshened up" the pole by painting it garishly before shipping.

Traditional objects and poles were scattered all over the world, some with complete, some with incomplete, documentation. It took extraordinary efforts to ship heavy totem poles, but new American and Canadian railway lines and steamship connections helped to ease the task. It has been reported that collectors received about one dollar per inch (about 40 cents per centimetre) for a totem pole. If we use the price of gold to measure inflation (gold was about $11 an ounce then) the equivalent of a typical pole (18 to 25 metres tall) would be about $25,000— for the collector alone.

Some small amount of good did, however, emerge from the period. The impact of the non-Native influx was so great and the stoppage of traditional ways so complete, that today Native people search through museums and ethnography collections for old songs, old stories, old totem poles, old masks, and for confirmation of their traditional standards. Without these collections, much could have been forever lost.

Though mortuary figures, greet figures, and totem poles were never worshipped, early missionaries misunderstood their role and, in many cases, encouraged Natives to chop, burn, and destroy their treasures. Many that remained were snapped up by museums in the collecting frenzy of the late 1800s.

Tall

Short

Frontal

TOTEM POLES come in many shapes and sizes.

Tall freestanding poles are usually commissioned to mark a special occasion and require years of planning. The design is conceived through a collaborative process under the direction of one person, and the pole is carved by a team of apprentices under a master carver. The concepts behind tall totem poles are important, and there are layers of meaning intermingled among the figures. Status among totem poles is determined by the reputation of the chief carver, the number of consultations held with elders, and the size of the ceremony accompanying the raising. The first

freestanding poles were probably made by the Tsimshian people along the Nass and Skeena Rivers.

Short totem poles, the work of one or two carvers, illustrate a single story or one heraldic crest. This pole is the crest of a member of the Beaver clan. Its meaning can be summed up in a sentence or two. Raising ceremonies for short poles are simple affairs. Any pole, no matter how diminutive, rates a raising and blessing celebration in proportion to its size and importance.

Frontal totem poles were once carved into the load-bearing post holding the main beam of a longhouse. When height

became an issue, techniques changed. For at least 200 years, frontal poles have been constructed from separate logs, taller than the house, placed separately against the front or side of the structure. One of the original types of poles, especially popular among the Haida, these totem poles were once owned by the chief and families who occupied the home. Their presence served to announce the prestige and origins of the clans inside. This pole includes a ceremonial entrance at its base.

Greet Figures, or Welcome Poles, are based on the very first types of totem figures. Originally placed as memorials in graveyards or on beach landing sites

Greet figure

House board

Mortuary

to attract the attention of passing paddlers, today they stand at the entrance to parks, institutions, museums, or special areas.

Some greet figures have their arms outstretched; others stand arms down. A few are less human-like and feature more animal features. As their name implies, they substitute for a welcome mat, standing ever vigilant at attention and watching passers-by. This greet figure is covered with several markings.

House boards are quite rare. In their original environment, they would not have been free-standing as is the one shown here. House boards were located inside or outside the long-

house as decorative panels along the walls.

Ten to twenty of these panels decorated the inside or outside of a bighouse. House boards were particularly popular among the Coast Salish people. In previous times, this group carved a few totems, but specialized in greet figures and house boards. This particular carving was reproduced from an 1898 original and depicts a person with the power to mesmerize bears.

Mortuary poles are easily recognizable by the large panel that is said to have fronted a three-dimensional box. Said to contain the bleached remains of a high-ranking person, the box

was mounted high on the pole. It is difficult to ascertain if any of these poles actually held human remains. Even in archival photos showing newly made poles, funeral boxes seem to be missing. However, this style of construction is known as a mortuary pole and was developed among the Haida.

In native stories where these types of poles are featured, a group of friends of the deceased stands watch every night over the bones. One by one, they abandon their duties until only one person is left to defend against grave-robbers. This person then encounters the spirit of the deceased.

Roused to action by tourists who viewed the deterioration of totems alongside railway tracks, the Canadian government underwrote a restoration project in the late 1920's

Isolated Preservation Efforts: 1870 to 1940

As early as 1873, Dr. Israel Wood Powell, first Indian commissioner for British Columbia, toured coastal Native villages aboard the gunboat *Boxer.* Sensing the academic feeding frenzy about to accelerate, he strongly recommended the province of British Columbia begin an immediate collection of native art and artifacts. The plea fell on the deaf ears of a cash-strapped government. Powell was also the first to have misgivings about native Canadian items being removed to American institutions. This too met no response.

In 1889 the *Art,* Historical and Scientific Association was founded in Vancouver. Its mandate was to collect dilapidated poles, move them to Vancouver, and restore them. Evolving into the *Vancouver Museum Society* of today, this group was responsible for acquiring most of the present-day poles on display in Stanley Park.

The upper Skeena River was the site of another preservation effort. Roused to action by tourists' complaints about the serious deterioration of the remaining poles visible along the railway tracks, the federal Department of Indian Affairs, National Parks, National Museums, and the Canadian National Railway undertook the first project of its kind to restore the poles along the river. Between 1925 and 1929, about 90 percent of the poles—60 were salvageable—were restored at Hazelton, Hagwelget, Kitwancool, and Kispiox. They were re-erected (at that time), facing the railway tracks, as tourist points of interest.

A few other western Canadian conservation efforts took place between 1935 and 1940.

CNR steamships were authorized to bring intact totem poles free of charge to Prince Rupert, BC. That community began an official city-wide totem pole collection, still enjoyed today. During that period, several poles were added to Vancouver's Stanley Park

The Northwest School of Native Art is a Native-run school for Native artists and carvers founded in 1969. Many of its graduates have gone on to outstanding careers. One way to recognize the graduates of this school is their characteristic stylized depiction of a hand.

collection. A few old totem poles were erected in Victoria on a vacant lot on the corner of Bellevue and Douglas Streets, a site that later became Thunderbird Park.

Sensitized to the deterioration of native sites in Alaska, a few voices were faintly heard. As early as 1918, US Judge James Wickersham started a

fledgling movement to preserve the remaining totem poles at Port Tongass. At the same time, James G. Steese, president of the Alaska Road Commission, tried to stop road builders from destroying totem pole sites. Beginning in 1926, Alaskan forestry worker and concerned citizen Charles Florey wrote to government officials lamenting the deterioration of native sites. However, no significant action was forthcoming until 1937, when the US Forest Service commissioned a census of poles and community houses. Between 1938 and 1940, the Forestry Branch subsequently spent $200,000 on a Civilian Conservation Corps. With the help of many local Native people, they restored a number of important Alaskan totem poles and structures. The refurbished poles stand today near Ketchikan. As part of the same program, the first true Alaskan potlatch since 1900 was held in 1940 among the Kake Natives of Wrangell. At the potlatch, of-

ficially hosted by both Chief Shaikes and the US Forest Service, several new poles were commissioned. Because one was called Barbecue Raven, suspicions were roused that the new poles had lost some of their traditional meaning.

Except for isolated instances and a few funded preservation projects that employed Native and non-Native carvers—traditional totem pole building among the Natives of British Columbia and Alaska was virtually defunct for almost 50 years.

Revival of the Old Ways: 1949 to 1965

Though there were a few exceptions, after 1890, totem pole construction and the ceremonies associated with it became increasingly dormant for almost 50 years. One famous carver, Charley James (1867–1938) of Alert Bay continued to teach his children and grandchildren the old ways. His poles were recognized in academic circles and among art aficionados. In the 1940s, his granddaughter, Kwakiutl, Ellen Neel (1916-66), one of the few recognized fe-

Thunderbird tops one of several historic totem poles on display at Vancouver's Stanley Park. The first of these poles was collected about 1889; the original of this particular one was acquired in 1927. It was replicated in 1988.

Left: Blankets stacked high are for gift giving at an early potlatch in Alert Bay. As well as blankets, quantities of food, dishes, canoes, and other trade goods were given away. This Kwakiutl community continued its practices in spite of a Canadian law banning "gift giving." Right: In 1921, sewing machine and furniture giveaways, so outraged authorities, that they came in and seized all the community's potlatch masks and traditional regalia.

male totem pole carvers, lived in Vancouver and made a meagre living producing high-quality miniature totem poles. About this time, academics at the University of British Columbia (UBC), planning Western Canada's first museum dedicated to native artifacts, realized the lamentable state of Northwest Coast native heritage-art. Obtaining a small grant in 1949, they hired Neel to restore seven salvaged totem poles. There was no standard technology or methodology for restoration work, and the task was daunting. Neel began work and solicited the help of her step-uncle Mungo Martin—another Kwakiutl student of Charley James. Within a short time it was ascertained that duplicating totem poles using new logs was more satisfactory than attempting to restore old poles through intense labour. Martin quickly eclipsed Ellen Neel, and his fame spread. He became the "Father of Totem Pole Revival" in the twentieth century.

Neel continued her efforts

for native art, training her son David Neel until his untimely death in 1960. She collaborated with anthropologist Marius Barbeau and spoke at numerous university convocations and conferences. In addition to thousands of miniatures, Neel went on to carve full-sized poles for Stratford, Ontario, and the Museum of Copenhagen in Denmark. She carved five major poles for western Canada's Woodwards' stores. Though she conceived and helped to promote the idea of Vancouver marketing itself as "Totemland," her valiant first contributions are usually overlooked. In spite of the overwhelming publicity her famous relative Mungo Martin continued to receive, and in spite of the fact that she predated him and acted as his mentor, Canada Council turned down a request to fund her totem pole projects as late as 1960. She died in disappointment in 1966.

By 1947, several circles of academics, including E.W. Hamber, Chancellor of UBC, were aware that potlatch tra-

ditions and accompanying totem pole making were in serious decline or completely lost. Beginning in 1950, a UBC academic committee and provincial anthropologist Wilson Duff spearheaded a three-year pro-

To Commission a Full Size Totem Pole

The Copper Maker
Hunt Family, Box 755,
114 Copper Way
Port Hardy, BC V0N 2P0
(250) 949-8491

Hy'emass House
468 Island Highway
Box 883
Parksville, BC V9P 2G9
(250) 248-2423

Krentz Forest Products
Richard Krentz
Box 733
Campbell River, BC V9W 6J3
richard@krentz.com

Native Heritage Centre
200 Cowichan Way
Duncan, BC V9L 6P4
(250) 746-8119

ject to bring totem pole traditions back from the brink of extinction. Under the direction of chief carver Mungo Martin and his son David, a team of apprentices was assembled in Victoria. Their names still read like a "Who's Who" of native art: Bill Reid, Henry Hunt, and his son Tony Hunt. About 13 replicas of totem poles were produced and raised with appropriate ceremonies. Elders from outlying communities travelled to Victoria to perform traditional raising ceremonies. When funding ran out, the Victoria Times Colonist newspaper organized a community donation project. In 1953, a large ceremonial bighouse, officially named Old 'Naka'pankam', was built in the centre of Victoria and dedicated to Martin's family-clans in perpetuity. The elaborate and authentic potlatch dedication ceremony attracted elders from throughout British Columbia. The public almost stampeded the ceremonies, and anthropologists declared that a wealth of native dances and traditions, previously unknown, had been revived. The bighouse structure was constructed to shelter Martin's restoration work and to show gratitude for his contribution to the people of British Columbia and the world.

With replication projects well underway, it was not long before the subject of tall totem poles returned to the forefront. In 1956, Martin and his team raised the world's tallest totem pole—38.9 metres (127 feet, 7 inches). Located in Beacon Hill Park, Victoria, it was

designed to pay tribute to Canada's World War II Native war veterans. With word of the world's tallest spreading through the media, orders for totem poles poured in from museums, governments, and private citizens. Mungo Martin and his team carved two identical centennial poles. In 1958, one was presented to Queen Elizabeth II and the British royal family in London, England. They are exactly 100 feet (30 metres) tall. The Colony of New Caledonia, later called British Columbia was established in 1858. The duplicate centennial pole was raised in front of the Maritime Museum in Vancouver.

In 1959, David Martin, Mungo's son and chosen successor, accidentally drowned. Martin remained stoic. After giving the situation considerable thought, he decided to turn over what would have been his son's legacy to the provincial museum. In addition to masks, personal regalia, and totem poles, he also donated his copper, symbol of his authority and wealth.

Having revived excellence in native arts and having taught several other apprentices, Martin passed away in

In the late 1930s, the US Forest Service dispelled disparaging rumours of the day that a slave's bones were buried at the base of old totem poles. Many original poles were dug up, but no trace of bones was ever discovered. Today, a silver dollar is buried at the base of some poles.

1962. His body lay in state and was returned with great ceremony to his chosen place in Alert Bay. Soon after, his community began plans to construct the world's highest totem pole in his honour. To continue Martin's work in Victoria, Henry Holt was appointed chief provincial carver. The Alert Bay band fulfilled its plan in 1980, when a 53.7 metre (173 foot) world-record pole was raised.

The Canada Council posthumously awarded its highest medal to Martin in 1963, but plans for various memorial plaques in Vancouver and Victoria never came to pass. The provincial government eventually commissioned a small 9.8 metre (32 foot) memorial pole in his honour in 1970. It was raised in the Alert Bay cemetery where he is buried.

Public Appreciation Grows: 1955 to 1975

Meanwhile, Martin's apprentices began several projects of their own. Bill Reid, a soon-to-be famous Haida artist, first travelled to Haida Gwaii in 1957 to assess the poles there. He then returned to oversee a three-and-a-half year university-sponsored project with Namgis artist Douglas Cranmer. Together, they oversaw the construction of the native-style houses and carved totem poles now in place outside the Museum of Anthropology in Vancouver.

During the 1960s and 1970s, commercial businesses, government bodies, and other institutions began to appreciate the uniqueness of this ancient art form. Scores of poles were commissioned. The Boy Scouts of Canada commissioned a pole for their new headquarters in Ottawa. Woodwards' stores employed Ellen Neel to construct five poles for their stores. The province of British Columbia commissioned 11 Native carvers and their assistants to build 19 poles to be placed along BC highways and at ferry terminals. The Canadian government commissioned poles for some of its embassies and

Miniature Totem Poles

MINIATURE TOTEM POLES are sold in souvenir stores. However, they play a greater part in the totem pole tradition than many tourists suspect. Before a full-sized pole is constructed, miniature versions are carved to check out the effect and to gain the approval of the chiefs and elders who have commissioned the pole. If the carver has inadvertently carved an offending story figure or crest, the figure can be modified before a full-sized rendition is made. These mini-poles have value on their own.

In past times, when a totem pole was destroyed, it was sometimes replicated secretly in miniature form, to remember it before time obscured its features. Many traditional Haida totem poles claimed by destruction or decay are known only by miniature argillite poles carved in remembrance of them.

This archival photo shows pole carver Opitsit, a carver about 1920, working on miniatures that will be approved and later carved into full-sized totem poles.

as national gifts. Juneau, Alaska, marked its 1972 centenary with two authentic poles.

During this era, new precedents concerning the collecting of native art were established, and these are still followed today. No longer can totem poles be expropriated. In 1958, for example, Gitksan village chiefs allowed some of their poles to be removed to a museum for preservation. Their conditions stated that the poles be replicated and returned. They were. A totem pole, on display at Expo '70 in Osaka, Japan, was returned after the fair was over. At the time of this writing, the Museum of Civilization in Ottawa is unable to persuade Kitwancool village elders to relinquish the famous Hole-in-Ice pole, one of the oldest in the world.

A renaissance in excellence emerged. To encourage young carvers, the Kwakiutl Arts and Crafts Foundation began in Alert Bay. Young artist and carver Robert Davidson returned to his roots and in 1969 raised the first new pole in Haida Gwaii in 50 years. This was followed in 1984 by a Bill Reid pole. An accredited school of Northwest Coast native art was founded in 1969 near Hazelton. Museums throughout the world re-evaluated their totem pole collections and realized the extent of their treasures. The Museum of Anthropology at UBC opened in 1962 with a compre-hensive collection of indoor totem poles. Later the museum hosted a year-long exhibition of Norman Tait totem poles. In Kake, Alaska, a tall pole, 45.7 metres high (150 feet high), was raised, and a number of older poles from around Alaska were assembled at the new Ketchikan Heritage Centre. 'Ksan, a re-created native village in northern British Columbia, opened with great fanfare.

New names emerged as proficiency increased: Norman Tait (Nisga'a Tsimshian), Richard Hunt (Kwakiutl) and Calvin Hunt (Kwakiutl), Bob Neel—son of Ellen Neel (Kwakiutl), Joe David (Nootka), Art Thompson (Nootka), Robert Davidson (Haida), and Nathan Jackson (Tlingit).

Public appreciation for totem pole carving gradually increased, but sadly, several impostors began to take advantage of the public's overall lack of familiarity with the tradition. True totem poles are the work of Northwest Coast Natives. Totem crests and the retelling of narratives are the prerogative of Native carvers and their apprentices. Completed poles must be raised and blessed with appropriate ceremonies conducted by Northwest Coast band elders. However several "fake" totem poles made both by Natives and non-Natives from completely unrelated traditions continued to appear in public

Tall totem poles are important for boasting rights, but they do not photograph very well. This 38.9 metre (127 foot, 7 inch) pole erected in 1956 at Beacon Hill in Victoria, once held the record as the world's tallest totem pole. As of 1995, it is surpassed in height by two taller poles—one in Kake, Alaska 45.7 metres (150 feet), and the tallest in the world at Alert Bay at 52.7 metres (173 feet).

places—usually outside British Columbia and Alaska.

Unfortunately, opportunistic artists using chain saws continue to turn out "totems." Several people who never knew Mungo Martin masquerade as one of his trainees. One unsanctioned pole carved by an Ontario non-Native man (married to an eastern Canadian Native woman) stands prominently in the centre of Banff, Alberta.

Native Art by and for Native People: 1980 to Present

In the 1980s and 1990s Natives gradually began to operate their own tourism establishments. Realizing the public appeal of their own art and heritage, Natives opened their Kwagiulth Museum and Cultural Centre on Quadra Island. The abandoned Ninstints (Skungwaii) village was declared a World Heritage Site and is administered by the Haida. Kiks'adi Totem Park and Saxman Village in Alaska were dedicated. To celebrate the momentous occasion of raising the world's tallest totem in 1980, Alert Bay's collection of potlatch treasures, confiscated by the government in 1922, were returned to the Kwakwaka'wakw people. A great ceremony followed. The treasures remain on permanent display at the U'mista Cultural Centre. In 1983, Duncan, BC, declared itself the City of Totems and set up a perpetual totem pole carving regime among the Cowichan people. They in turn opened the Native Heritage Centre, complete with a carving shed to shelter totem pole carvers year-round.

How Old are Totem Poles?

Elder Robert Good views a replication of Hole-In-Ice, a pole once reputed to be one of the oldest "still standing".

TOTEM POLES ARE generally constructed from untreated cedar logs. Though cedar is resistant to insects and fungi, the effect of weathering is relentless. After 70 to 100 years battling the elements, totem poles tend to decay and fall over. An old totem is the responsibility of the descendants of the family that erected it. Until that family can afford to commission a duplicate, the spent totem may lie on the ground. It has not been forgotten. When arrangements are completed, family carvers are appointed. The old pole is carefully moved to a carving shed, such as the one pictured, and a duplicate is made. If there are no talented carvers in the owner's clan, outsiders may be appointed. However, in that case, an appointed family member must "stand over" the hired carvers during every moment of the process. In the end, the re-carved pole becomes a symbol of honour for the family.

Thirty-nine properly dedicated totem poles stood in Duncan by 1994.

Museums have slowly instituted new policies. For example, the Museum of Anthropology in Vancouver loans out its artifacts to Natives for use during their potlatches, and many important items have been returned to the people. Museums throughout North America, including the American Museum of Natural History, are reviewing requests by native people to return all or part of their collections. In 1993, the Anglican Church of Canada made a much publicized return of its confiscated Kwakwaka'wakw treasures.

Northwest Coast native art continues its slow renaissance in the world outside the region. In Paris, in 1992, a major exhibition was mounted. A team of traditional canoeists travelled up the Seine River, and the art received widespread acclaim. Bill Reid's art and jewellry has increased 10 fold in value in less than a decade. The names of other native artists have become recognized in non-Native settings. In 1993, a statue designed by Bill Reid was placed in front of the Canadian embassy in Washington, DC, drawing outstanding and appreciative public reviews.

The quality and fluid lines of authentic Northwest Coast native art as it has evolved from the mists of ancient times to the present day continue to bring pleasure to onlookers. The art of totem pole building continues to be an important part of that tradition.

Two Haida houses on the grounds of the Museum of Anthropology at UBC represent a family dwelling and a small mortuary chamber. The poles were constructed by Bill Reid (Haida) and Douglas Cranmer (Kwakiutl). In former times, a typical Native village consisted of about 50 such buildings, each housing a dozen or so families.

Alert Bay, the final resting place of Mungo Martin, is a predominantly Native community. It is home to the U'mista Cultural Centre housing treasures of the potlatch, a totem pole that was one the world's tallest totem pole, and a Big House.

Built in the style of a Kwakiutl bighouse, this building in the centre of Victoria was dedicated by potlatch in perpetuity to Mungo Martin and his family clan. It is only opened during ceremonial periods, but can be viewed from the outside at anytime.

2. Totem Pole Symbols and Ceremonies

A glint of sun hints at Thunderbird's traditional power to control lightning

Totem pole symbolism is intimately linked to the kinship system of the Northwest Coast. The family relationship, as defined among members of a group, is called its kinship system. The familiar Western kinship system of mother-father, brother-sister, uncle-aunt, niece-nephew, sister-in-law and brother-in-law, is based on European convention and law, as well as on blood relationship. The common system of surname transfer, for example, is generally based on the recognition of the father's or one parent's paternal line of ancestry. In the recent past, a woman used to automatically drop her own surname at marriage and take her husband's. Lately, some children inherit double surnames—including the wife's birth surname. This is based on an evolving, but yet imperfect, method to interweave the maternal line into a paternal system. However, if after two generations of hyphenated surnames, the last name becomes unwieldy,will the female line name be dropped?

Northwest Coast tribal groups before contact had evolved a kinship system that featured some of the same rules as the European system and some of their own conventions. As individuals did not have surnames as we know them, and with four or more marriages common among women, the transfer of prerogatives based on parentage was complex. For example, the system of passing names was generally through the maternal line, and inheritance or wealth was often passed from a man to his nephew, not his son. Names were often assigned rather than transferred. Certain names were split in half

Natural

Painted

Feathering

FEATHERING IS A special technique much favoured by several Native artists. Done with a small adze, the "chipping" technique covers the entire surface and takes a great deal of time. However, the finish lends a richness to the surface, particularly evident as the pole ages. Feathering is an "optional extra" on particularly valuable poles, adding a patina of quality to the pole.

Grain blasting is a new technique just beginning to come into favour among artists. When a particularly attractive grain is revealed, gentle sand blasting is used to bring the grain into high focus. Here, the blasting was skillfully done, after the feathering details were first masked off.

A natural smooth finish remains a favoured technique. Without any paint at all, the natural carved shapes and wood grain of the pole come into high focus. When a pole is new, its natural colour is yellow-blond or reddish-blond. Cedar wood ages in about two years to a characteristic silver-grey. It is normal for

Grain Blasting

poles to crack with age, and various techniques are now used to periodically fill the cracks and sand them smooth. Some people prefer poles with natural cracks.

Painted surfaces were once popular but are becoming less fashionable. Inspired by the bleached remains of old poles, modern artists increasingly use coloured paint only as accents or not at all. The Kwakiutl people

continue to produce poles with the greatest number of painted and add-on pieces. Painted poles also suffer the effects of weathering and need frequent repainting if they are to appear new and bright. Some say they like the weathered look, and others enjoy a totem best when it is freshly painted.

and one syllable transferred from one name and one syllable from another. Though lineage was generally based on the maternal line, occasionally a complex combination of the two lines could be arranged. For example, in some groups the inherited privileges of a wife's ancestors could be passed as a gift to a husband by his wife's father. However, the mother's genealogy was always paramount.

Phratries are the political-kinship divisions of people tied both by blood and by the need to band together as a tribe for protection. Banding together to form a community, these people then begin to claim descent from a common ancestor. In other cultures, specifi-

cally among the Scottish or the Irish, such groups are known as clans. For describing the Kwakiutl people only, Franz Boas, an early anthropologist, coined the term *numaym*. In this book, the more widely used terms of "phratry" and "clan" are used interchangeably for all Northwest Coast kinship divisions.

Phratries or Kinship Groups

"Phratry" is an academic term used for tribal people along the Pacific northwest coast. Kinship groups associate together and claim descent from a common ancestor, who may be non-human. Phratry association can be passed by blood or by assignment during a public ceremony. For example, a per-

son not previously a member of an Eagle phratry could be declared a member and thus claim descent from Eagle. This is somewhat similar to our present-day adoption system.

Phratry associations were not only based on blood relationships but also on the need for certain families to see themselves as intimately related for the purposes of defending themselves against common enemies and of working together to collect food and provide a comfortable lifestyle. The addition of political or protective connections to the family line is not widely recognized in Western society. However, it was essential among Native groups. Each of these groups of people

Linkages: Nature and Totem Art

THE FIRST FORCES that inspired carvers to create the characteristic shapes seen in Northwest Coast native art are lost in the mists of time. But a walk along the beaches and in the rainforests of Alaska and British Columbia conjures up shapes and figures that may show a link between the land and the art of the people. Powered by a small degree of imagination, it is possible to see beached logs taking on animal forms, knots in trees with faces, shadows playing into shapes very much like those seen in the works of master carvers. The appeal of Northwest Coast art may be that it strikes a deep cord of recognition and seems to show humanity's oneness with nature. The figures shown here are a Gitksan totem rendition of Mosquito and a strongly reminiscent piece of driftwood.

Commemorative

Pride

Story

TOTEM POLES ARE MORE than stories. Hidden among the figures are layers of intertwined meaning. One figure may represent more than one thing. For example, Bear may be a family crest, the telling of Bear's story, or a lesson to remind Native people that self-sacrifice is desirable. Furthermore, the whole pole may be a memorial to an honoured elder or serve as testimony that the carver has, for example, overcome an addictive habit.

Narrative Story Rights or Story Figures

Certain figures appear on totem poles as a symbol of the owner's rights to tell the stories or sing the songs associated with one's phratry or family kinship. These figures include the popular Bear, who represents a common story with wide rights of telling, or Raven and

one of his cycle of stories. Southern bands carve poles with more narrative figures. Today, stories are told freely without much regard to traditional rights. The story pole shown here illustrates the famous story of Bear-Mother. (See Chapter 3 for a complete telling of this story.)

Remembrance of Heroic Events

In some cases, the figures on totem poles are meant to recall a heroic exploit, the sufferings of a brave person, or a memorable disaster such as a flood or volcanic eruption. Since the events are primarily important to Native people, they are not always familiar to outsiders. However, the photo here shows a commemorative pole erected to a modern non-Native hero, Rick Hansen, a wheelchair athlete who wheeled around the world over a two-year period raising millions of dollars for spinal cord research.

Pride in One's Native Heritage

The outstanding art form that totem pole carving embodies has advanced to the point where modern artists carve poles with loose relationships to past practices. Tribal styles are liberally interpreted; stories are given new twists; phratry crests are included with or without rights. While purists may express concern about these practices, there are so many talented artists and so many wonderful stories full of life and movement that the natural progression of the art form is toward the expression of the tradition as pride in one's heritage. On these poles, the artist simply declares what the pole represents. There is less need to resort to strict protocol. The photo here shows a totem pole expressing various native concepts of transformation, some heraldic figures, and the need for cooperation between people.

Ridicule/Amusing

Ridicule, Shaming, or Amusing Acts

In a few cases, totem poles contain figures meant to shame the owner of the pole. If the carvers were not paid, if the family owed debts, or if protocol was breached in a serious manner, the rules of totem pole carving were deliberately broken. In most cases, outsiders cannot see the breach, but Native people can. To greatly insult the owner, a figure might be visibly carved upside down or embarrassingly naked. Ridicule poles are rare because the owners generally do not raise them. In a few cases, mistakes or figures are added simply to create amusement. The photo here shows a humorous figure, in this case, meant to amuse rather than ridicule.

Mortuary or Memorial Remembrances

Among coastal First Nations, totem poles continue to be raised at a great potlatch in the years following the death of an influential elder. The totem serves both as a remembrance for the family and an announcement of their rights. Traditionally, northern bands carved more totem poles serving strictly as memorials than their neighbours to the south. A few included mortuary boxes constructed to hold the last remains of the deceased. Shown here is a mortuary pole, which in the old days would have fronted a mortuary box.

Kinship Rights or Heraldic Crests

Certain figures appear on a totem pole announcing the right of the owner to display a symbol associated with their moiety relationship

Heraldic

or phratry. Outsiders sometimes compare these to clan surnames. These kinship symbols were passed by blood through the maternal line or were granted to a person during public ceremonies. Heraldic crest figures include various mythological beings such as Siskiutl, Copper Woman, and Moon Crest, as well as various animals such as Double-Finned Whale or Giant Beaver. Northern bands carve poles with more heraldic crest symbols and fewer narrative figures. The heraldic pole shown here consists almost entirely of the Frog heraldic crest repeated over and over.

Mortuary

Here dancers pose in the costumes they use for dancing ceremonies and rituals stretching late into the night. Young initiates receive affirmation of the traditions of their ancestors.

claimed similar attributes, symbolized by displaying certain animals or mythological figures.

Moieties

Moieties are the largest phratry divisions in a tribe, or approximately the largest "half and half" divisions among bands. For example, all the members of one tribe might belong to either the Wolf or the Raven moiety. Additionally, there may be 50 to 100 subdivisions under the two major divisions. Each of these subdivisions has the right to display certain totemic figures, but not others. Each person is allowed to display their major moiety symbol and a variable number of the submoiety symbols based on kinship and property rights. To the present day, when outsiders ask a Native person about his or her Native name

or clan associations, it is a difficult question. Most Natives give simplistic answers to what is a very complex situation. Others leave their clan associations and rights for their elders to sort out. "Ask my auntie," they say.

Titles

Titles are a series of ranked positions that were generally inherited through the maternal line. Interest in property came through the male lines; kinship rights through female lines. Titles could be earned by an individual who had an encounter with a supreme being or in recognition of a contribution to the group. Among the Kwakiutl people, for example, during the nineteenth century, there were about 900 titled positions. Titling rules were complex. Native people operated under an oral (not a written)

tradition. Thus there was no official "rights and privileges registry office." Rather, the granting of a title was symbolized by the right to display certain totemic figures and the process verified by an official witness. These powers, privileges, and interests in property were then symbolized by the right to

a) be called a certain name and claim descent from a certain phratry

b) perform certain dances and sing certain songs

c) tell certain stories

This bestowing according to the laws of kinship was then symbolized by displaying sanctioned totemic figures on one's dishes, clothing, weapons, and totem poles. Great offense was taken if anyone displayed a figure to which they had no rights.

This armorial bearing has meaning within the British heraldry system. The arms are registered with a central body that approves the design and sanctions the right to officially display it. No two registered coat of arms are identical, and each symbol has meaning. In many ways, this practice corresponds to the traditional native system for sanctioning totem figures.

Exogamic Marriages

Exogamic marriages are the custom of marrying outside one's own close kinship group. This is widely practised around the world, but the definition of who is "close" varies. There were strict exogamic rules among the various phratries along the Northwest Coast. However, these rules arose from a combination of heraldic crests and property rights. Therefore, one was sometimes entitled to marry a person who might be considered taboo in Western society, and by the same rights others were off-limits under the totemic system who were considered un-related in the Western system.

The System of Witnessing

All this complex granting of names, rights, privileges, and the symbolism associated with it had to be recorded. In a society without a written language, this could be a complex task. Therefore, a whole system of witnesses and witnessing arose to keep track of the kinship, marriage eligibility, and property transference. At each public ceremony, a witness or a group of witnesses was formally appointed for each portion of the ceremony. These groups of persons were entrusted with the duty to watch carefully, memorize a portion of the proceedings, and give a first-hand accounting of the granting of a kinship right or property rights whenever asked to do so. The witness-person or witness-group could be called on at a later date to verify that a privilege had indeed been publicly granted. To be certain that the witnesses paid strict attention during the

Common Practices

The practice of associating under animal symbols is not exclusive to Native people. Even in Western society, groups of people band together for common purposes under animal symbols. For example, the Fraternal Order of Eagles, the Lions Clubs International, and the Elks Lodges consist of like-minded people who help each other and society, especially

those most in need of protection—its underprivileged. Cities, municipalities, and individual families often commission an armorial bearing or a coat of arms that symbolizes the characteristics identified with the city or family; these are strictly defined under the British or German heraldic systems.

long ceremonies, they were given lavish gifts. This was to attract their attention, to thank them, to perpetuate a sense of belonging, and to compensate them (in advance) should they ever need to travel back to bear witness in a dispute over property or kinship.

Rights, Symbols, and Heraldic Crests

Ethnographers commonly accept totemism as a type of social organization that defines lines of kinship and records them for posterity. Under totemic rules, there are definitions about whom one may or may not consider as a marriage partner, based on who has and who has not the right to claim association with certain totem figures. In ancient times, there were also little-mentioned (and imperfectly followed) practices within totemism, such as certain taboos against eating one's totem animals.

Within the totemic or phratry system, a totem animal or supernatural figure is variously regarded as the blood-line parent of the group or, in certain circumstances, as having granted rights to the group by association. Exogamic marriages were sanctioned, and

Prominent symbols displayed on native ceremonial clothing and on totem poles serve to announce a person's rank, prestige, and kinship relationships.

Hints for "Reading" Totem Poles

1. Create an imaginary line from west to east across the northern tip of Vancouver Island. Totem poles *north* of this line consist mainly of heraldic crests with a few story figures carved in for contrast. Totem poles *south* of this line are mainly story figures with a heraldic crest or two interwoven among the figures.

2. Older totem poles show more heraldic crests and fewer story figures.

3. Modern totem poles show more story figures and fewer heraldic crests.

4. Modern poles commissioned for non-Natives are concerned with art, line, and form, and tend to consist of story figures. The artists and carvers may or may not include their personal heraldic crests.

5. Totem poles commissioned for Native use are careful to follow heraldic crest rules as well as strict story lines.

members of each clan were considered to have certain rights, privileges, and prohibitions stemming from their phratry associations. The etiquette and protocol based on rights was complex. When a large gathering of many clans met, there were hundreds of conventions to be observed. It was easy to inadvertently insult someone. As a result of the regulations and privileges within the totemic system, planning for a potlatch was as complex as the modern equivalent of planning protocol for a visit from British and Arabic royalty—at once.

Each right, privilege, and kinship association was publicly noted by displaying certain heraldic crests or narrative figures on one's privately owned articles and, in later times, the carving of those symbols onto totem poles. Because a person spent a whole lifetime accumulating rights and heraldic crests, sometimes the sum of one's symbolic figures might not be carved onto a totem pole until after one's death. Then the pole with its heraldic crests and figures served as an announcement of the departed's total family-line rights to be passed on to future generations.

Still later, other minor symbols were intertwined into totem poles. These include statements of ridicule and commemorative stories of great events. In modern times, the passing of phratry rights among Natives is being revived. However, totem pole figures carved for non-Natives and public institutions do not represent phratry rights but are the evolution of an outstanding art form.

The crest of the exclusive Vancouver Club symbolizes its links with Canadian history (the beaver trade), its association with British royalty (the crown), and its perceived prestige (the subdued effect of the total crest). In some ways, this corresponds to the traditional native system and the prestige associated with displaying certain totemic figures.

The Potlatch

The potlatch celebration is the oldest and most important festival among the Natives of the Northwest Coast. In previous times, it sustained their ranking system and brought a sense of order to the system. In the present day, it perpetuates a sense of belonging.

A gathering to which people were invited to share food for a betrothal or a birth was called a "feast". A potlatch is a gathering where people were called upon to bear witness to a myriad of legal matters and to receive gifts. In early times, potlatches might be held once a decade. After European contact, with the greater dissemination of trade goods and the emergence of a nouveau riche class, potlatches might be held every two years or so. There was no fixed schedule for potlatching. Elders called a potlatch when they were ready.

Much misunderstood by outsiders, the potlatch was a time of affirming social rank, taking care of important legal matters, establishing a sense of order in the society, and providing for the redistribution of goods from the few to the many in order to impress one's rise in station on others.

Preparation

Once the long preparation period leading up to a potlatch was almost completed—all the goods were in transit, the artworks and totem poles were carved, and the gifts were ready—the elders held long meetings to establish the legalities to be dealt with and protocol to be followed. Finally, about three to six months in advance, runners were sent out to neighbouring villages. All who were invited were expected to attend along with an unlimited number of guests in their entourage. It might take more than one day for all the guests to arrive. Ceremonies were held as each canoe appeared, and welcome dinners were generous.

Legalities and Witnessing

As the potlatch commenced, the first items on the program were long opening speeches and the acknowledgment of protocol among the guests. Then began the lengthy settlement of legal matters. Witnesses or groups of witnesses were officially appointed to remember each portion of the events. In case of later dispute, these witnesses could be called to bear witness to the matters and testify as to how they were settled. After the witnessing system was in place, the legalities began. This could take up to three weeks in early times, but after contact, potlatch ceremonies were held more frequently and the elders could handle all the matters at hand in about three days.

There were a variety of legal matters:
• Betrothals were announced.
• The goods and property of

Preparing for a potlatch was a complex undertaking. Here, a shipment of gifts barely impresses invitees who are arriving by canoe for the start of an Alert Bay potlatch about 1910.

the dead were fairly distributed among the survivors.
• Outstanding disputes to claims of property and rights were settled.
• New property rights were granted.
• Rewards for outstanding ser-

Tongue Linking and Tongue Thrusting

THE ORIGIN OF TONGUE linking and tongue thrusting on totem figures and in other native art is obscure. Particularly well-represented in the Haida tradition, the meaning is bound up with a transfer of power between two entities. In murals and argillite pipes, the tongue of one figure extends deep into the throat of its linked entity. The two figures are bound together in an act of transfer. Single tongue-thrusting totem figures may be a variation of tongue linking and may show that the entity has power to spare. It could also be a variation on lip plugs *(labrets)* once worn by upper-class persons to show their rank. It is fascinating to note that New Zealand Maoris display tongue thrusting prominently in their dances. However, no traditional link has ever been established between the two cultures.

Today Native people display their heritage through the use of native symbols. However, strict traditions are no longer followed and most designs are simply an expression of native pride.

time is unprecedented in Western society and unusual even among the Native people of North America. Among all these legalities, the most important were the distribution of property and the granting of rank through names and the rights to symbols. The potlatch may have arisen because coastal groups were among the least nomadic of all Native groups, having a settled society and patterns based on an assured food supply—the harvest of salmon. Whatever the potlatch's origins, the societal sophistication these ongoing performances brought to the people was severely disrupted when outside authorities suppressed this gathering ceremony. It is easy to imagine the chaos that might result if all these legalities were suddenly disrupted in our own society.

The Evening Program

During the evening sessions, there were legalities and affirmations intertwined with entertainment. New initiates were introduced or inducted into the system. Traditional songs were sung and dances performed by groups with

vice were given.

- Old disputes over previous potlatch legalities were settled.
- A person who was disabled received formal compensation.
- New names were given out according to advancements in rank and title.
- New births were acknowledged.
- Important marriages were performed.
- Injustices or "civil" cases were settled.
- Scores were settled.
- Minor criminal acts were punished.

- Memorials like totem poles were raised to announce new rankings or to honor the deceased.
- Memorial ceremonies for the dead were held.
- New longhouses were dedicated, named, and blessed.

Additionally, certain elders might pontificate with long speeches on some virtue or issue of importance to them. During this time all the guests, especially witnesses, were well fed and were entertained nightly.

The concentration of all these legalities and ceremonies into one condensed period of

Bear sitting upright

curred very late at night. In early times, the rites of the old ways were passed to the young through solemn rites of anthropomorphism and anthropophagy. The resulting dance frenzies sometimes involved injury to members of the audience or even the death of a slave. This was all done in great secrecy.

Acts of Gifting

The part of the ceremony that most offended and startled the sensibilities of outsiders was the lavish gifting to witnesses and guests. To thank people for their witnessing services and to demonstrate the rank and prestige of the person holding the potlatch, gifting became ever more elaborate. Before contact, gifts might include boxes and inlaid box lids, carved feasting dishes, grease ladles, ivory carvings, and baskets. After contact, the Hudson's Bay blanket was the dominant gift and the standard against which all other gifts were measured. For example, a copper was said to be worth 5000 HBC blankets. Gifting might include canoes; sewing machines; hundreds of pots

and pans; thousands of HBC blankets; foodstuffs like flour, sugar, and hard tack biscuits; and copious quantities of trade goods. Gifting went on and on, with wave after wave of goods being carefully bestowed on people according to their rank. Everyone received something; rich people received more than others. Today money, such as stacks of $10 bills, are given out among the other gifts.

Before the 1800s, when potlatches were rare, long periods passed while the elders paid artisans to prepare items for the celebrations. After the 1800s, however, when potlatches became more frequent, women were compelled to go to town and there find work. They sent money back to their chiefs and elders. Some of the services the women offered were degrading and thus offensive to the missionaries. This often unstated fact is one reason the potlatch was opposed by religious authorities.

Another little discussed fact are the three prominent anthropologists of the day who spoke out against the potlatch at the time they became illegal. Their reasons were quite underhanded. When an arrest was made under section 116 of the Indian Act, authorities threatened to throw elders in jail. Rather than humiliate their superiors, a village was sometimes given the option to sell all their regalia, masks, and paraphernalia to the three eagerly waiting anthropologists.

Breaking the Copper

By far the greatest prestige among all gifts was bound up with the copper. The copper-breaking ritual was concerned with wealth as a commodity

rights to them; new songs and dances were given out. Puppet shows and slight-of-hand tricks added a surreal dimension to the evening festivities. Famous figures such as Dzunkwa (Cannibal Woman) might suddenly appear and expect to dance and be fed along with the other guests. Thunderbird was known to shift shape and come as a human to some of these nightly entertainment sessions. Siskiutl, the sea snake, called up from his underground lair, arose to cast long shadows in the light of the brightly burning fires.

During these sessions, the most dramatic ceremonies oc-

(like money) and was designed to elevate one chief's status above all others.

Chiefs owned coppers made in a characteristic form, something like an incised shield. Coppers were well known and had names like Bear Face or Making-the-House-Empty-of-Blankets. A copper was broken off, one corner at a time, and pieces presented to high-ranking persons. As a chief broke his copper, he destroyed the integrity of the design. The ritual then became a game of one-up-manship. If a visiting chief was offered a piece of copper, it was mandatory for the guest to offer a larger copper piece of higher or at least equal value back to his host. Any rival unable to do so was humiliated before the community and the wealth of the potlatch host well established. Records show that one potlatch host even threw his copper into the sea—in the ultimate gesture of high-status nonchalance.

Rivalries arising from this ceremony created the most enduring "humiliation" imbalances between groups. The humiliated chief was doubly motivated to mount his own community potlatch and restore his dignity by even more gifting and a larger copper ceremony. The intense rivalries involving coppers ceased about 1920, although they still play a ceremonial role in potlatches.

The Place of the Totem Pole in Potlatch Ceremonies

Against the background of the kinship system and its affirmation during potlatches, the totem pole was the visible symbol of the passing of rights

All societies and groups announce their affiliations by the use of flags, symbols, trademarks, and logos. Here, the flag of British Columbia intermingles with the Double-Finned Killer Whale totem crest.

Record-Making Totem Poles

TOTEM POLES naturally lend themselves to comparisons. Shown here is "Cedar Man," the world's thickest totem pole.

- World's Tallest Totem Pole: 52.7 metres (173 feet), Alert Bay, BC
- World's Second Tallest Totem Pole: 45.7 metres (150 feet), Kake, Alaska
- World's Thickest Totem Pole: diameter of 1.8 metres (6 feet), Duncan, BC
- World's Oldest Totem Pole: Hole-in-Ice, 1860   Kitwancool, BC
- World's Largest Collection of Old Totem Poles: Ketchikan, Alaska
- World's Most Comprehensive Indoor Display: UBC Museum of Anthropology, Vancouver, BC

As another wave of gift giving begins, potlatch participants watch as the helpers await the signal to begin distributing flour, sugar, and hard tack biscuits.

in a society with an oral tradition. The totem pole affirmed the narrative stories, the history, the culture, and the rights of the people.

Carving totems was the formal method of announcing those family rights and prerogatives that had been passed to them during the potlatch ceremony.

Modern Potlatches

Potlatch ceremonies continue among all coastal groups today. In some cases, Natives have developed a sense of humour about the outside world's curiosity. Outsiders require written invitations. So many strangers were turning up uninvited, they sometimes outnumbered the Native participants. One famous skit performed at modern potlatches

entitled "Rent an Anthro" is a tongue-in-cheek chiding for families who have not yet been investigated by their very own anthropologist. Art pieces and totem poles continue to be produced for potlatches at a gratifying pace. Most impor-

tantly, potlatches have adapted to the modern need for creating cohesiveness among Native people of the Northwest Coast.

Totem Poles: Legitimacy

TOTEM POLES: legitimate or not?

- Poles made by Northwest Coast first people for their own bands and people continue to state the owner's family rights.
- Poles made by Northwest Coast native people for outsiders are an expression of their native culture, heritage, and pride. On rare occasions, at the discretion of the carver and the band, these poles bestow certain rights on their

new owners. Most do not.

- Northwest Coast native people periodically grant the right to carve totem poles to visiting apprentices from bands outside the region.
- Poles made by non-native people, chain-saw artists, and unauthorized natives from "non-totem" traditions are imitation totem poles.

1. Totem poles are first planned in meetings between the artist/carver, the pole's commissioning body, and elders (if necessary). A place to carve the pole must be arranged and a lumber company consulted to provide a "clear" tree. Clear trees have few knots or imperfections. In some cases, the carver will travel into the woods to inspect the tree before it is cut down and occasionally, the carver personally fells the tree. Meanwhile, design preliminaries are made on paper and the design is repeatedly brought to its owner for approval. The design is finalized.

2. Sometimes a small model of the pole is carved to see how each figure will be integrated into the total design. Workers prepare blocks to elevate the log to a convenient horizontal height for the carvers to work without bending. Totem pole carving tools, custom-made for the purpose, are sharpened. All is made ready for the arrival of the log.

3. The tree is delivered to the carving shed, where it is debarked and tested for imperfections. Some trees contain hollow centres that lie undetected. These must be uncovered and repaired, or the log is rejected. Once the outer bark is removed, the wood is given a cursory smoothing. Sometimes elders are called in to say prayers over the log and ask it to release its spirit to the carvers.

4. The artist or master carver draws the outlines of the approved design onto the wood and the sapwood is feathered away. The tree is very fragrant at this time and its heady aroma fills the carving shed. Carvers now begin to sing songs to the log and talk to it as they work. The figures begin to emerge from the wood.

5. Most carvers begin from the bottom of the pole, moving gradually to the top. Bottom figures are carefully detailed because observers see these figures close-up. The flow of the design between characters is sometimes revised from the original plan. The master carver chops out the rough forms, then discusses the overall concept with each of the new apprentices as they arrive.

6. Morale is a matter for the master carver, who is expected to inspire the team. A team of apprentice carvers now arrives to help with the carving, and they begin to work under the guidance and inspiration of the master carver. The bottom end of the pole and important details are finished by the master, while the outlines and top end of the pole are completed by the apprentices.

7. Finally, the shapes are refined and the final form of the finished pole is evident. Various finishing techniques are applied, attention being paid to each detail: the tail of Beaver is cross-hatched; each eye is carefully delineated. Carvers work in teams of one to three persons and take frequent breaks. Small poles take two or three months; large poles up to eight or nine months to finish. The duration of the project is determined by the length of the

pole and the money available to pay the carvers.

8. Paint is applied, if necessary, and arrangements for the raising ceremony are made. Incising and other details are added with the approval of the master carver. At

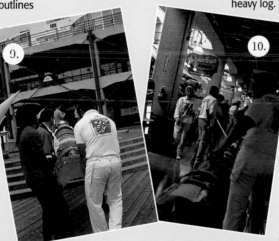

this point, some poles are washed and cleansed. Finally, the pole lies in wait for its moment of glory—the raising ceremony.

9. On its second-to-last day in the horizontal position, the pole is moved near the place where it will be raised. In some cases, the

time to move the pole is carefully determined. Those who are asked to move the totem, in its last private moments before it becomes public property, consider it an honour to transport the heavy log. These are among the last moments the pole still "belongs" to the people who made it.

10. As the pole is moved to its staging area, it sometimes makes the strangest journey of its life. This "pole on wheels" takes a shortcut through a public market to its final destination in an outdoor public square. In modern times, with the curiosity of the public so intense, private ceremonies for Natives and invited guests are sometimes held the night before the official raising. The "real" blessing is made at that time.

11. The elders gather, the crowds assemble, and the beating of the drum announces that the formal raising ceremony is about to begin. People slowly take their places. There are no set procedures for totem pole raisings. All totem pole raising ceremonies differ according to the elders who conduct them, the traditions of the particular tribe, and the prestige and protocol required for the owners of the pole.

12. In this particular ceremony, the women were first asked to circle the log, touching it with live cedar branches. Women, it was explained, bring the ever-lasting spirit of "life" to the totem figures. Then the carvers and some of the men were asked to join in. All brushed the pole with live cedar branches to awake its living spirit. This particular feature is not a part of all pole raising ceremonies.

13. In all ceremonies, however, special homage is paid to the carvers. In this ceremony, they were asked to dance and sing their own songs for the pole. As they danced, the story behind the pole was told to the assembled public. Outsiders then begin to understand and appreciate the inspiration behind the pole. Other ceremonies may differ in how they show honour to their carvers.

14. Many speeches are made and the pole's final moments in the horizontal position draw to a close. As all the participants draw close to the pole, the speeches, songs, and invocations become increasingly solemn. It is both a joyful and a solemn moment.

15. The pole is hoisted aloft by a team of dancers and helpers. At some raisings, spectators may be pressed into service. A parade forms and the pole is slowly moved to the exact place where it will stand. In this way, as it moves, the totem pole becomes part of the people.

16. In some ceremonies, more invocations are said and more songs are sung. Here, helpers strain while final preparations are made for the final hoisting. Because this pole is small, it was simply dropped into a metal ring holder. In early times, a sloping pit was dug and poles were gradually eased into the upright position using overhead ropes and backfill.

17. Today, modern technology is a bonus for moving larger poles into position. Cranes and sky-hooks make the job an easier

one, though the starting and stopping of the machine can create anxious moments for the spectators.

18. Even with the help of modern technology, the carvers and their teams of helpers always seem to experience some worrying moments. There are ongoing concerns, both for the safety of the surrounding public, who invariably press too close, and for

the carver, who, like the anxious bride at a wedding, is asked in detail what he or she wants at every step of the pole placement.

19. Small poles rate small ceremonies; important poles rate important ceremonies. The status of

a totem pole is bound up with the reputation of the carver, the prestige of the owner, and the number of elders and appropriate dignitaries the raising ceremony attracts. Small commercial poles such as this one being raised in front of a gift shop rate appropriately sized ceremonies.

20. After the upright totem pole is in place, dance ceremonies take place. The carvers and their families are given places of honour, as are the owners of the pole. The Native people then give out gifts, usually fresh apples and oranges, to the crowd as a gesture of thanks for bearing witness to the raising of the pole. The feasting that follows goes on late into the night.

3. Identifying Totem Figures

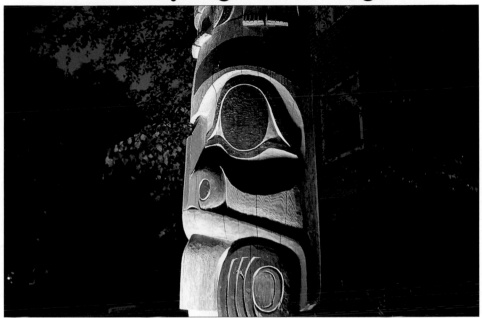

Bear glows as the sun sets

In 1909, John Reed Swanton, an anthropologist, identified and catalogued 62 Haida heraldic crests. A few years later, in 1916, Franz Boas, a collector and an ethnographer, reported on 99 different Tsimshian heraldic crests. Each of these crests is carved onto at least one totem pole. Since that time,

many potlatches have been held and the number of heraldic crests sanctioned among all Northwest Coast Native nations has increased. Therefore, the figures listed alphabetically in this chapter do not cover every heraldic image and story figure carved onto every totem pole in British Columbia and Alaska. Instead, the listings are representative of some of the common figures a viewer is likely to encounter. Any given totem pole is likely to display several additional figures whose exact meaning is known only to the carvers and the owners of the pole.

For a century between 1840 and 1940, early anthropologists and ethnographers travelled among the people collecting objects and recording their family stories and songs. The stories condensed in this section are derived from early recorded accounts. In each case, an academic researcher interviewed Native subjects who recounted stories as they were handed down from their grandparents and great-grandparents. Some of these stories, therefore, may stretch back to precontact times. Many are the retellings of stories originating long before that. In the decades since these stories were first collected, they have been subject to "re-editing" to reflect current thinking. Particularly in recent years, traditional stories are being completely reinterpreted. With the exception of Thunderbird's story, which is modern, the stories in this chapter are the retelling of compilations based on early recorded accounts freely given to museum and

IN THE TIME before this, it was berry season and the women ventured far from the village to harvest the crop. Among their numbers was a princess, daughter of a great chief, who was unaccustomed to such work. The spoiled girl begged her father to let her go adventuring with the women, and he reluctantly agreed. All day she had problems. First, she stepped in bear excrement. Breaking a taboo specifying that no Bear should be insulted, she complained long and bitterly. Her companions fell silent. When it was evening and time to return home, her headstrap broke three times, her basket spilled, and she fell behind. Frantically seeking her agile companions, she encountered a handsome young man who offered to carry her basket and take her to his village before dark. She was pleased to go with him.

After a long walk, the two arrived at an odd village inhabited by people wearing bearskin garments. The princess was introduced to her companion's father, the Bear-Chief, who treated her kindly. While the slaves were preparing her dinner, Mouse-woman crept to her side with pertinent information on her predicament—the princess was a prisoner of the Bears, who would shortly assume their normal appearance. Mouse-woman advised her to cooperate and gave her procedural hints to avoid becoming their slave. (These rituals form a significant part of the story, but they are not related here.) The princess followed Mouse-woman's directions to the letter.

Back in her own village, her people were grief-stricken. Her four brothers and a dog set out to find her. Each killed many bears during his search, and the first three brothers were unsuccessful in their quests.(The brothers' adventures form a significant part of the story, but they are not related here.)

Unlike the heroine in *Beauty and the Beast,* the young woman easily adapted to living with Bears manifesting in their own shape and size. Bear-Prince asked for her hand. They were duly married, with a proper ceremony, and soon she gave birth to Bear twins. She was a devoted mother, and the boys grew quickly. When it became known how many Bear brethren were being killed in her name, her caring Bear husband decided to move the family to a more secure location. They travelled high into the mountains where they lived quite happily. The Bear-Prince performed certain rituals to insure their safety. (These form a significant part of the story, but they are not related here.)

When the rescue team under the direction of her fourth (and weakest) brother was finally sighted, the princess pressed her fingerprints into a snowball and rolled it down the mountain to attract their attention. Her rescue was at hand. Just before her husband, the Bear-Prince was killed, he asked to sing a dirge by which he might be remembered. His wish was granted and as he died he pulled the bearskins from his children, making them manifest in their human form.

Bear-Mother and her offspring returned to her human village, founding the first generations of the Bear clan. There are supplementary stories about her unhappiness and the family's periodic return to the Bear's village.

Bear represents a spirit of noble self-sacrifice

ing Bear characters are performed in many First Nations groups and both Bear-as-a-foster-parent and Bear-as-a-spouse stories are common. Bear medicine is known to have curative powers, and some shamans can transform themselves into Bear. Some of the oldest artifacts recovered on the West Coast include a shaman's crown made of bear claws.

Bear is not a mere animal to be admired or hunted, but also a semidivinity. Its ability to form a link between humans and the spirit world is a common thread between many cultures. Bear stories are very ancient.

Bear's Appearance

Totem Bear is distinguished by its ears (if present), snout, teeth, eyebrows, and paws. The ears are flattened in an inverted U-shape, often containing smaller decorations or little bears inside. In earlier times, its teeth were not always defined, but modern carvers show Bear teeth with prominent incisors. Eyes are well defined and feature eyebrows. Many Bears sit upright, and Bear-Mother holds a human-looking child in her arms. If Bear's animal nature is uppermost, its paws are shown, its claws are well defined, and smaller figures appear on its pads. If the shape-shifting abilities of Bear are illustrated, it has a combination of human features and animal-human appendages.

university researchers.

Cautionary Note: These stories are not suitable for children. They are the oral stories that give meaning to the kinship systems of Northwest Coast Native people. They contain many stated or implied concepts suitable for mature minds.

Bear and Bear-Mother

Bear and Bear-Mother are prevalent players in many mythologies. In the western world, bear stories such as *Why Bear has No Tail* and *The Three Bears* are passed on through fairy tales. However, Bear is a more serious creature in aboriginal cultures. Bear ceremonies, as well as Bear images, are particularly well developed in Siberia and among the Inuit people of the North. The Ainu of Japan pay extensive homage to Bear. Mimetic dances and ceremonies featur-

"…That I may…take hold of your left paw…to inherit your power of getting easily with your hands the salmon that you catch."
— *Kwakiutl, Chant to a Black Bear*

Bear's Personality and Habits

Bears live in families, and have brothers, sisters, chiefs, slaves, wives, and husbands just as people do. They live in social communities, understand religious taboos, love their children, hold marriage ceremonies, and mourn the death of their brethren. They hold meetings and seek each other's advice. Like humans, they go out hunting in the day, have meals, celebrate life events, accept and give gifts, and value copper as a commodity. They venture out on occasional slave raids but they capture humans—not other Bears. Unlike humans, Bears build their hearth fires with very wet wood because they have the ability to keep it alight; dry wood goes out when they ignite it. They hibernate in winter. Most Bear households shelter a wise talking rodent, Mouse-woman, as a sort of permanent houseguest. She knows all their deepest secrets.

Bear Powers

Like all other animals, Bears have the power to take their skins off and appear as human beings do. Most of the time, however, they prefer their own form. They are quite perceptive in knowing when human hunters are after them, and a few have a precognition of their own death. Of great importance is their ability to mate with humans, who then give birth to twin offspring. The children grow from babyhood to young adolescence in record time, can assume either parent's form at will, enjoy the company of either their mother's or their father's families, and exhibit the best abilities of both Bears and humans. However, Bear children marry humans. It is these offspring who founded the first "human" Bear clan families.

"Welcome, friend, Throwing-down-in-One-Day, you Tree-Feller, for you have agreed to come to me…that you may give me your ability to work…for nothing is impossible for you to work at."
—Kwakiutl, Chant to Beaver after It Has Been Killed

Today, these phratries have expanded to include new heraldic crests such as Bear-of-the-Sea, and many phratries have inherited the right to carve Bear as a story figure. In the strictest totemic tradition, kinsfolk never ate or hunted their totem animal. In practice, this was sometimes circumvented by claiming the animal killed was only a "natural" bear, not a Bear.

Bear's Relationship with Humans

Though humans are their enemies, Bears appreciate human awe. They are aware of the taboos and ceremonies humans hold in their honour, and they are annoyed when humans utter insults against their dignity. Both groups tend to

This pole represents Beaver's return as a revered animal in place of its former status as rival.

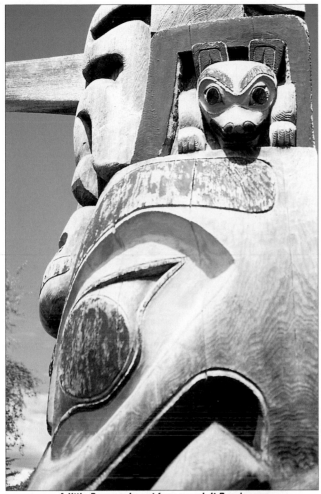

A little Bear peaks out from an adult Bear's ears

heraldic crests signifying the right to trade in pelts was a serious matter. To this day, the Beaver is Canada's national emblem.

Native Beaver clans on the West Coast can trace their origins to about 1830, when the Hudson's Bay Company became active in fur trading west of the Rockies. Adapting HBC's royal emblem, several members of the Eagle, Double Eagle, Salmon-eaters, and other phratries began to display Beaver as one of their own crests. This signified their right to trade in pelts. Since trapping was their livelihood, it would not be proper for Beaver crest holders to claim they were descended from the animal. Who would kill their kinsfolk for a living? Instead, Beaver's crest was passed to humans for avenging a great wrong.

Beaver's Appearance
Beaver is identified by its prominent front teeth and a paddle-shaped tail. Never located on the back of the pole, the tail is folded upward in front of the body. Tails are textured with crosshatching or other markings. Beaver sometimes holds a stick or an arrow in the horizontal position in its front paws or in its mouth. The race of Giant Beavers with enormous tails is well known to humans. Some have extra animated faces on their tails and paws. When they die, the faces die with them.

Beaver Personality and Habits
Like their ordinary animal counterparts, Beavers are active, build dams and lodges, and raise their young. A race of Giant Beavers lives in communities with powerful chiefs,

avoid each other except during berry season when they uneasily frequent the same berry patches. Rank-and-file Bears marry their own kind, but occasionally a Bear-Chief's son falls in love with a human female—always a high-ranking chief's daughter. He is a faithful husband and a dutiful father in spite of being fully aware of his in-laws' murderous intents. His offspring eventually go to live with the human side of their family. Their progeny are humans but are

intimately related to Bears and therefore owe Bears special homage and favours in return for their special powers.

Beaver

Beaver is a story character and heraldic crest among Native people who engaged in the fur trade. With the arrival of Europeans, the search for fur-bearing animals was so enhanced that hunting areas became the subject of great rivalries. The desire for wealth created a productive industry. The system of speaks their own tongue or human languages, and composes their own songs. They are very deliberate in constructing huge dams, diverting rivers, and digging tunnels. They are cunning in their ways and clean in their habits. Unlike Bears, they are reclusive and care little about humans or their insults, except in one instance. They are short tempered if humans question their craftsmanship, engineering skills, or weapon-making abilities.

Beaver Powers

Like other animals, Beaver can appear as an ordinary creature or it can remove its skin and temporarily take on a human form. Giant Beavers are a race of beings with tails so large, one slap can start an earthquake or cause a lake storm. In certain circumstances, they can slap their tails and become invisible. Beavers keep their own supplies of sharp arrows and spears on hand should they ever be attacked. They use their teeth to sharpen these weapons and employ fine crafting techniques not generally recognized by humans.

Beaver's Relationship with Humans

In general, Beavers rarely fraternize with humans, preferring to keep to themselves. When humans invade their territory, they commit frightening acts, even to the point of murder, thus warning humans to keep their distance. To discourage human habitation, Beavers have been known to tunnel under a human village. No one suspects their undermining until the ground collapses. In one case only, a human kept Beaver as a pet. In the presence of all humans except for its owner, it assumed the size and habits of an ordinary beaver. The man became so fascinated with its alternate form that he neglected his own family. This caused jealousy among his relatives.

Hidden between the lines of the following story are hints about the rivalries between clans. The underlying story is about who has legitimate rights to use the "new" Beaver crest. Within the double meanings concealed in all native stories is the story of wars between competing humans. Read the story first as it is written and then read it a second time substituting "a rival group to the Beaver clan" for the word "Beaver."

Birds

Beaked birds from several species appear prominently on totem poles. These include Eagles, Woodpeckers, Hawks, Owls, Ravens, and several powerful mythological birds. The highest in rank is the Thunderbird.

The Eagle plays an esteemed role within many Native groups. All North American aboriginals use eagle feathers and down for ceremonial costumes, headdresses, and decorations. Mimetic Eagle dances echoing the raptor's soaring flight, wing movements, pinched looks, and dis-

Thunderbird over Whale

appearance into the clouds are performed everywhere in the world. Eagles are noted for their longevity, swiftness, keen vision, and the dizzying heights to which they soar. The Bald Eagle, for example, is the national emblem of the United States.

Thunderbird is an extremely powerful Eagle. A very old conceptual form appearing both in Asia and among various tribes of North American Native people, the image of a "bird that thunders" is prevalent from the Northwest Coast to California and as far south

A Composite of Beaver Stories

IN THE TIME BEFORE this, a household slave was ordered to awaken the chief, who did not arise at his usual hour. The chief's body was covered with a mat, an arrow was sticking out, and the man was dead. Nobody in the village knew how it happened or for what reason. The nephews of the chief extracted the arrow and saw that it was expertly crafted. They passed it round. Usually someone could identify an arrow by its markings, but this shaft was unknown.

After the funeral and rights of succession, a great feast was prepared. Everyone from far and wide was invited to come. In this way, the nephews hoped to gather information about their uncle's murder. Many people examined the shaft, but their information was of little use. One guessed that the Beavers had made it, but this suggestion was met with catcalls and insults. It was laughingly agreed that Beavers are awkward, and stupid, and they could not possibly possess the skill to create such a fine weapon.

One of the guests, a stranger wearing a beaverskin garment, took particular interest in the general derision. When the murder weapon was again passed round, the stranger spoke in a quiet voice, "This finely crafted arrow belongs to my brother."

At this pronouncement, the unknown man pulled his garment up over his head, slapped something hard on the floor and disappeared —taking the arrow with him.

Immediately recognizing the creature as Beaver, the feasters gave chase. As they neared the pond, they saw two huge Beavers sunning themselves. One had an arrow in its teeth, but both creatures quickly dived into the safety of their lodge. The villagers now agreed it was Beaver who had killed their chief.

The people prepared for war. (These rituals form part of the story, but they are not related here.) Gathering up shovels and using poles as levers and stakes, they burst the Beaver dam.

There are several versions of the battle that followed. Some say the Beavers were slaughtered on the spot; others say it took time until the Beavers came to inspect the damage. During the wait, as guards kept watch, the Beavers ambushed and killed some of the humans. Some say the Beaver wives managed to escape into a secret whirlpool.

All the stories agree on two vital points. First, one Beaver was covered with living human faces. As he died, all of its faces died with him. And the Beaver-Chief was so powerful, it took several men to subdue him. The spears of the Eagle clan struck true, but the spear of another warrior broke. Since the Eagles actually killed Beaver, they claimed full rights to use its crest; had the spear of the other not broken, that clan too would have had right. However, in the heat of battle, one spear faltered. That was a fact.

After the war, the chief and council decided to move their people to a more secure location. Beavers are powerful beings and their revenge can be severe. The stories diverge on the number of villages, their locations, and relocations. The villagers split up and resettled some distance away.

Many years passed and there seems to have been a continuing struggle over who was entitled to display Beaver's crest. Then one day, in one of the villages, a great clap of noise rumbled through the earth. When the people ran in panic, they fell into collapsing pits. Many were killed. Unknown to the inhabitants, the Beavers had undermined their village with hundreds of tunnels. The collapsing ground triggered nearby landslides that blocked the salmon run. A great famine followed.

Near another resettled village, the Beavers dammed a river, diverting the salmon. Another famine, another battle followed.

The stories go on to explain how the Eagle phratry used this period of famine and the subsequent disintegration of the social order to gain undisputed control over its use of the Beaver crest.

as Central and South America. Powerful Thunderbird also appears among Plains and Eastern Woodlands tribes. To many outsiders, Thunderbird is central to the concept of a totem pole. However popular its image may be, Thunderbird is not mandatory.

There are several other equally important beaked creatures who also appear as heraldic crests or characters in stories. Thunderbird's closest relatives and companions include Kolus, Hok Hok, Hawk, and Eagle.

Beaked Birds' Appearance

Thunderbird has an eagle-like beak, talons, claws, feathers, and raptor-like eyes. In previous times, Thunderbird always sported curly antenna-like ear bobs, while Eagle had no ears.

Today, carvers create Thunderbird figures without antenna or distinguishing ear pieces.

Kolus (also spelled Kulus, Quolus, Q'olus) is the younger brother of Thunderbird and its kin. Covered with dazzling white fluffy down, he sometimes becomes overheated—especially when he visits swampy, humid areas. He used

A Modern Thunderbird Story

IN THE TIME BEFORE this, a giant Whale the size of a mountain came to inhabit the oceans offshore. Its appetite was enormous, and each time it was hungry, great storms arose. The seas were swept clean of all life. The salmon did not return to the rivers and humans began to starve. One of the great chiefs climbed a cliff overlooking the ocean and begged Whale to leave. Whale ignored him. Still Whale fed and there was no food for humans. After a time, a council was called. Chiefs from far and wide tried to decide on a course of action. Leaving aside their personal arguments, they climbed the cliff. Though they used their best abilities, no matter how they begged, Whale ignored them.

Finally rituals were performed to invoke a greater power. (These rituals form a part of the story, but they are not related here.) No one would dare call on Thunderbird directly by name. Weeks went on, the famine deepened. One afternoon, black storm clouds swept in from the ocean. An invisible presence was felt among the people and a voice echoing with a thousand swirling winds demanded to know why it was summoned. When they

made their request known, the presence was quiet. Finally it asked, "What will you do for me?" The chiefs consulted among themselves. Perhaps they could hold a series of potlatches in its honour? But they had been starving for many seasons, there was no food, and the people were depressed. A potlatch some time hence might not be the best compensation when the threat needed immediate attention.

Finally, one of the lesser

chiefs had a bold idea. They would adopt a crest, authorize rights, and build totem poles in honour of this presence. Its image would appear above all others, on top of every pole in the land for all time.

The presence was pleased, and in a terrifying fury, it made itself visible. The awesome form of Thunderbird materialized from out of the storm clouds, lightning flashing from its eyes and talons, ear-shattering thunder rolling from under its wings. Thunderbird flew over the inlet and snatched up Whale in a single swoop. Stories diverge as to the ending of Whale. Some say Thunderbird ate Whale as usual; others say Thunderbird dropped Whale and it turned into a mountain still visible near present-day Duncan, BC.

Whatever the ending, Native people have kept their word. Thunderbird is seen topping many a totem pole among all cultures and many nations. And Whale is often seen, head down, right beneath.

Kolus is the square-headed brother of Thunderbird

Gull are rare depictions. Mosquito has a beak-like proboscis and is not a bird at all.

Beaked Birds' Personalities and Habits

Each beaked creature has supernatural strength, great dignity, and noble character. Thunderbird, Kolus, Hok Hok, Hawk, and Eagle are the royal family of the skies. Living in comfort, somewhere in the sky, with the usual complement of slaves, little is known about their personal life. Thunderbird does have a wife. The Natives of Siberia speak of female Thunderbirds who fly into a rage when humans ridicule the nakedness of their legs. Thunderbirds and their kind speak in several tongues, read human thoughts, and hold ceremonies of their own. They engage in wars with forces beyond the scope of human knowledge.

When Thunderbirds are in an area, lightning flashes and thunderclaps follow. Occasionally, human foibles annoy them and it is whispered that a Thunderbird, in a fit of rage, once tore a human to bits. Humans consider it expedient to invoke them only when necessary.

Thunderbird is sometimes sighted swooping down on a whale and lifting it aloft. This is its prey, which is consumed with great gusto high on top of mountains. Remains of whale bones found in the mountains are evidence of a Thunderbird's kill. Occasionally, it takes several Thunderbirds to lift particularly enormous whales.

Thunderbird has one archenemy. A ferocious horned underwater sea snake called

to sport ear tufts too, but they are often squared off today.

Hok Hok (also spelled Hokw-hokw or Huxwhukw), is also known as Koskimo, Khenkho, Crooked Beak of Heaven, or Cannibal Bird. Hok Hok features an enormously elongated beak. Hok Hok is really a form of Raven and features prominently in Kwakiutl Hamatsa dances. One of three cannibal birds, Hok Hok is an agent of the cannibal who lives at the north end of the woods. Its beak is useful for cracking skulls and sucking out eyes. It

is one of the cannibals that escaped the purge when the transformer rid the world of these creatures.

Unrelated birds (and beaked nonbirds) occupy a separate position in the hierarchy of totem characters. Owls are associated with the dead and darkness, while White Owl is a family crest along the Skeena River. Raven has a heavier looking beak than his raptor cousins and is part of a separate cycle of stories (discussed later in the chapter). Loon, Heron, and

Siskiutl (SISK-yu-til) almost matches its heavenly foe in power and cunning. Siskiutl also has the ability to change size and transform itself into a giant Woodworm. Thunderbird uses lightning to rip open trees in order to search for this manifestation of its enemy. The image of a huge eagle figure clutching a snake-like creature in its talons is prevalent in many cultures all the way to South America.

Kolus, the younger brother of Thunderbird, has a lot to prove. Noted for lifting heavier loads than its older brothers, it has been known to help humans raise their heavy big-house beams into position.

Eagle is the equivalent of an earl or a lord, reigning among his fellow birds, but in status, a little closer to humans. As a bird of warning, it often plays a helpful role and has been known to rescue people about to fall off cliffs. In its viler persona, it steals babies. Occasionally groups of Eagles will get together and attack a whale, lifting it out of the water, just as their cousins the Thunderbirds do. Closely associated with Thunderbird, Eagle possesses many of the same traits.

The Hawk figure is much like its Eagle cousin, but more prone to taking on human form for long periods of time. During these periods it is known as Hawk-man or Hawk-woman. Known to interact freely with humans, Hawk also likes to eat mosquitoes—and mosquitoes are intimately

Basic Shapes

Split U

U design

Totem pole art contains characteristic shapes which give it a unique look among all other aboriginal art. By observing design details, one can see several unique shapes: the ovoid, the elongated U, and the split U, along with elongated shapes and circles.

Nested Ovoids

"Ovoid" is a unique term for a flattened oval shape that is intermingled, woven, and repeated in all Northwest Coast art. It sometimes appears on its own and sometimes is nested (as shown here) with additional ovoids or other shapes. With more squared corners than

Nested Ovoids

regular ovals, the term "ovoid" was coined about 1965.

Incised U

The U with a somewhat flattened bottom is also typical of the native art of the region. These forms are found in every possible orientation; right side up, upside down, and sideways.

The slightly off-centre orientation is a feel the Native artist brings to the work.

The Split U form is a variation of the regular U, and variable design mechanisms serve to divide the wide space between the two arms of the U. Split U's are common and are found in every orientation in Northwest Coast art. This particular split U, has a design flair on the bottom left corner, which is not present on all split U's.

These basic forms—the ovoid, plain U, and split-U—are part of the "alphabet", so to speak, of totem pole art.

linked to cannibal figures.

Hok Hok is a powerful bird, much concerned with its position as the central figure in a frightening human initiation ceremony called the *hamatsa*. A vital part of cannibal dances, Hok Hok oversees young human initiates sent into the rainy woods to starve. Returning weeks later to the warm longhouse, the initiates dance menacingly, threatening to eat the spectators. No matter what foods they are offered, they express a desire for human flesh. Hok Hok can crack open human skulls with its powerful beak. It enjoys brains as well as eyeballs. Its "hap! hap!" cry strikes fear into human hearts. It is good friends with Dzunkwa and Bookwus, well-known cannibals. Hok Hok is a manifestation of a flesh-eating Raven.

Raven and Mosquito are characters in separate stories, discussed later in this chapter.

Beaked Bird's Powers
All sky creatures can remove their feather cloaks, becoming invisible or assuming a human form. Thunderbird can readily read human minds. Best known however, is Thunderbird's ability to cause thunder and lightning. Various tribes offer different explanations. According to Tlingit stories, Thunderbird simply rustles its wings. The Haida say that lightning is caused by silver fishes hidden

among its feathers or, in other cases, by a fiery dart sent forth from its mouth to kill whales. The Kwakiutl say lightning originates from the twinkling of Thunderbird's powerful eyes and thunder from its flapping wings, or thunder is the sound of dead ancestors echoing in its wake. The Nootka people offer several explanations. Thunder is its voice and lightning flashes from its talons; light-

ning is the glint in its eye; its neck is a snake that breaks free and scatters into lightning bolts.

Beaked Birds' Relationship with Humans
These powerful creatures live in an unknown dimension high in the sky. While they have the ability to read human thoughts, like all aristocrats they are mostly concerned with their own affairs. They intervene only when approached by an important delegation or a high-ranking person who observes the correct procedures. Occasionally, they have been known to transform and come down as humans to enjoy Winter Dance celebrations. A few fortunate humans have benefited from their intervention during house construction. Beaked birds are excellent at lifting heavy roof beams into place. Like all immortals, they can easily grant wishes—if they choose. It is sometimes dangerous to invoke them when they are involved in their own disputes.

Though Kolus is the raptor most likely to lift house beams, some humans insist it is actually Thunderbird. Any group fortunate enough to receive their help has the right to display their crests. At times, these magnificent raptors will warn their own heraldic crest people of an impending death.

Hawk Woman

THE FOLLOWING Dzunkwa tale is a traditional account of Dzunkwa's powers and is not suitable for children. Besides the disturbing aspects of cannibalism, there are underlying themes of implied seduction.

In the time before this, the children of the village were playing outdoors. Clever Boy was by the side of the river when he discovered a log, so he and three companions floated away. After coming ashore, they were travelling deep into a dark forest when they suddenly noticed multicoloured smoke rising from a branch-covered hut. (The original story explains the symbolism of each colour within the smoke, but that is not related here.) No one was home, so they played with the interesting toys strewn about.

Suddenly, they heard a noise. A giant Dzunkwa was approaching, pursing her lips, cooing seductively, and offering the children a piece of red gum. Clever Boy was wary, but the other three were greedy. "Give us some gum," they demanded.

"Come," she said, "I will get you some." Collecting them up in her wide open arms, she placed them in her basket and took them to her hut. Sticking a piece of gum on the children's eyes, she knocked them out and went to bed. In one version of the story, her victims were slightly injured; Dzunkwa then took a stick, rubbed it along their wounds, and gave it to her own children to

suck.

The next day Dzunkwa awoke and began preparing for a great feast. She chopped wood, made a fire, heated boiling stones, and prepared bentwood boxes for cooking. Outside her house, she removed layers of hemlock branches covering a long cooking trench. This she began to fill with hot coals. (The dances, songs, and rituals she performs form part of the story, but they are not related here.)

In some stories, Mouse-woman next told the children about their predicament. In others, they were well aware. The children knew they must escape. In various stories, there are different escape scenes. Only one version is related here.

Clever Boy was sitting with his companions hunched on the floor in one corner of the hut. He called his companions together and they conceived a plan. Clever Boy began fiddling with a toy bow. He shot a toy arrow out the doorway. Telling his sister to fetch it, the young girl sauntered out the door. Once outside, she ran homeward as fast as she could. Casually, Clever Boy picked up another arrow and shot it through the door. His younger brother, then the third child, casually repeated the girl's actions. Just as Clever Boy was about to repeat his ploy and pretend to fetch his own toy arrow, dull-witted Dzunkwa looked around and became very suspicious.

Quickly, Clever Boy devised an alternate plan. "Can I help you fetch some water?" he asked. Yawning widely, looking tired and very confused, Dzunkwa handed him a large container.

As he was stepping outside the door, Dzunkwa suddenly realized her folly. Running outside, she screamed to Bookwus, who was just arriving to join in the feast. "Our good dinner has run away," Dzunkwa explained. Hearing this, Clever Boy quickly climbed a tree and hid.

Bookwus, the Wild-Man-of-the-Woods, set off after the trio. (In the original stories, an involved "magical flight" scene ensued, but that is not related here.) The three escapees dropped ordinary objects that turned into massive obstacles (for example a handful of pine needles became a thick forest) and temporarily delayed their pursuer. Coming at last to their own village, the children met a search party of warriors who arrived just in time to capture Wild-Man.

Meanwhile, deep in the forest, Dzunkwa was searching for Clever Boy. Though he was well hidden, she spied his reflection in a mirror-like pond. Looking up, she called seductively to him, "How is it you look so handsome?"

"I always put my head between two stones," he quickly replied.

"Then I will do so too," she said. "Come down and show me." So that she too can become handsome, the boy instructed her to fetch two heavy stones. On her return, she dropped them down. "Now, come and show me," she cooed.

Though it is not explained as such in the stories, it seems that in the act of fetching the stones, dim-witted Dzunkwa actually became caught up with the idea of becoming beautiful. The boy cautiously ventured down the tree.

"Now lie down," he said. The boy placed her head on one stone and told her to shut her eyes. He lifted the other stone and smashed it down as hard as he could. Her brains scattered everywhere.

Clever Boy quickly raced homeward. Meeting the search party, they combed the forest, found her hut, and heard the immortal Dzunkwa singing happily. The party of warriors set upon her. She and her companion were placed on mock-thrones and treated roughly. The village people discovered the glowing coal pit and finished preparing the very fires in which the creatures had planned to cook their children. With the flames leaping high, the warriors disposed of the giants. Cutting them into tiny pieces, they carefully dropped all the bits into the fiery pit. To make sure no single trace of the cannibals remained, the fires were stoked for four days and nights. Sparks and embers flew up, high into the skies, day and night, night and day. Little by little, overhead, a transformation occurred. The sparks turned, one by one, into swarms of buzzing, angry mosquitoes.

This explains why little mosquito is eager to taste your blood. And this explains why a squashed mosquito leaves little trails of gray "ashes".

Mosquito

A Composite of Mountain Goat Stories

IN THE TIME before this, the Mountain Goats were very angry because humans had been slaughtering them in large numbers. Many were killed for sport, not food; some were maimed for the fun of it.

One day some playful children caught a baby Kid down by the river. Imitating their elders, they made a fire and tried to burn it alive. Raven-Feather took pity on the little creature, rescued it, and kept the Goat hidden in his lodge. To heal its wounds, he rubbed a little fat on its burns and spread a little crimson salve around its eyes. When its strength returned, Raven-Feather took it back to its home in the mountains.

One day two strangers appeared in the village. Entering the chief's bighouse, they invited the whole village to a great feast. Everyone got ready, then followed the visitors up the mountain. When they came to a large mountain lodge, there was a sumptuous feast lying in wait. In one of the stories, the elders ignored their own children's warnings that their hosts were eating grass.

Without much appreciation for the feast, the villagers greedily gobbled up the delicious food. Some stories say they further in-

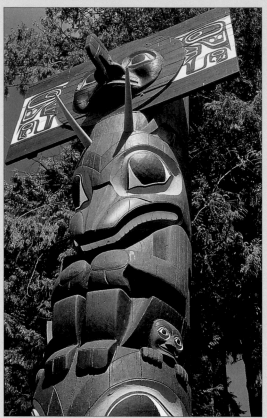

sulted their hosts by pilfering leftover food morsels and hiding them in their blankets.

While the guests were waiting for the after-dinner dances to begin, Raven-Feather observed the preparations. He noted that all the dancers wore goat-skin robes and mountain goat headdresses, and that they danced in an unusual way. One dancer had red circles around his eyes. In one story, this particular dancer approached Raven-Feather and instructed him to sit tightly against the wall; Raven-Feather quietly obeyed. In another story, the little boy was asked to sit at the place of honour. (The ensuing dances

and songs form a part of the story, but they are not related here.)

The leader of all the dancers had larger and blacker feet than the others. Unexpectedly, in the middle of one dance, he charged past the guests, jumped over the fire, and kicked a hole in the wall of the house. With all the tumultuous songs and loud drumming, the guests began to laugh. Once again, the black-footed dancer jumped over the fire, charged out through the hole, and kicked against a nearby cliff. As the guests continued to laugh, the bighouse began to shake, a landslide was released, and the whole mountain began to collapse. The dancers calmly resumed their normal forms and scrambled agilely down the rock face. All the guests were killed.

In the morning, Raven-Feather awoke in the middle of a landslide. A Mountain Goat with painted eye rings stood watch and tenderly reassured him, "Because you saved me, I also saved you."

In certain stories, the boy returned to his village to discover he has actually been away for 10 years. The new people living in the village accepted him warmly.

Cannibals and Mosquitoes

Anthropophagy arouses emotions that are very powerful. That it was long ago practised on the Northwest Coast is beyond dispute. Dzunkwa (also known as Tsonoqoa or Tsonokwa and in previous times called Black Tamanous), is the figure most associated with the practice. Occasionally, she was joined in her ravenous pursuits by several like-minded companions: Bookwus, a short-beaked man-eating Raven, and snapping Hok Hok bird. These four players with taste for human flesh strike fear into human hearts.

Several southwest native, Inuit, Siberian, and Russian mythologies depict a "giantess" or "witch" with a basket or cauldron who carries off children. The Dzunkwa story related here is part of a worldwide cycle of stories embedded in many cultures. In folktales such as *Hansel and Gretel, Jack the Giant-Killer, Baba Yaga, Odysseus and Cyclops, Tantalus and Pelops, Van den Machandelboom,* and *Die Kinder in Hungersnot* stories the hero outwits a dull-witted ogre that eats human flesh. There are similar stories in India, Africa, and southern Australia. Certainly not meant

to be a children's story, the Dzunkwa tale previous is a traditional account of this cannibal-kidnapper's powers.

Today, Northwest Coast Natives believe that cannibals left the earth a long time ago. However, among the Kwakiutl of Vancouver Island, dance simulations imitative of the practice continue to be performed each year. The flesh-eating creatures are believed to be monsters left over from the time when the Transformer rid the world of offending beings. Dzunkwa and her companions somehow escaped the purge.

Totem pole heraldic figures themselves were long ago linked with complex rules about who and what can and cannot be eaten. For example, Bear clan members usually cannot eat Bear, their kin. These taboos may stem back to earlier times and earlier practices.

The linking of cannibalism, Mosquito, and fire shows a keen appreciation for the annoying habits of the tiny blood-drawing insect. This link is shared with Romanian stories, where one tale says mosquitoes were created from the devil's pipe, and with a number of Filipino stories about mosquitoes carrying fire and becoming fireflies.

Dzunkwa's Appearance

Dzunkwa is a dark-skinned, human-like creature usually portrayed with round eyes, furry eyebrows (if present), pursed lips, and pendulous, drooping breasts. In recent times, political correctness has edited the breasts. Skin glowing in the dark, her hair (if present) fans out in all directions. Dzunkwas are numerous, but live solitary lives deep in the forest, on the outskirts of most Native communities. Also known as the Wild-Woman-of-the-Woods, her male counterpart is Bookwus, also known as Wild-Man-of-the-Woods, Pugmis, or Woodman. He exhibits many of the same qualities as his female companion but lives in an invisible house and attracts the ghostly spirits of the drowned to him. The pursed lips of both figures represent a kissing motion meant to attract little children with a "come hither" gesture reminiscent of calling a dog. Dzunkwa some-

Haida-style

Coast Salish-style

SINCE THE ART OF totem pole carving was revived in the 1950s, the personal style of individual artists has begun to dominate totem pole design. Today, Reid poles, Tait poles, or Cranmer poles display artistic forms characteristic of their makers. In turn, these artist-designers may or may not pay tribute to their own tribal origins.

Increasingly, modern totem poles are an amalgam of several tribal styles representing the best of several traditions overlain with the style of the designer.

In earlier times, during the Golden Age of Totem Poles, from 1830 to 1895, each band developed a characteristic style and individual carvers adhered strictly to it. There was little room for individual imprinting. The following descriptions represent ideals of traditional tribal styles and are only glimpsed in bits and pieces on modern totem poles. Today, there are many variations since totem pole carving primarily becomes a general expression of native pride, rather than a tribal-related form of expression.

Kwakiutl-style traditional poles are noted for brightly painted colours of white, red, green, yellow, brown and black. Heads are large and blank eyes stare straight ahead. Unlike other poles carved in one piece from a single log, Kwakiutl poles feature add-on bits such as sun rays, whale fins, wings, or beaks. Figures are rigid and stiff. Winged Thunderbird dominates the top of almost all Kwakiutl totem poles. This figure has greatly influenced the totem pole movement everywhere. Miniatures, souvenir poles, and totem pole drawings feature the characteristic open-winged, rigid, straight-staring Thunderbird, first made famous by the Kwakiutl people.

Kwakiutl figures represent supernatural beings, with frightening overtones, known to live hidden inside their houses or nearby in the forest. Traditional and modern Kwakiutl poles are narrative in nature—that is, they tell a story and illustrate it.

Modern Kwakiutl poles are somewhat more relaxed, the eyes have greater depth and the overall pole is not completely painted. Thunderbird remains perched firmly on top.

Tsimshian-style poles made by traditional people along the Skeena and Nass Rivers contain two unique features sometimes imitated by modern artists. The poles are typically unpainted and come in a variety of forms (not all forms are illustrated here). The Pole is unlikely to feature a pole-topping Thunderbird, and the dominating bird, if any, is usually a long-beaked woodpecker or a curved-bill hawk.

Several, but not all, traditional Tsimshian poles feature bands of small people compressed between larger animals. The largeness of the mythical figures dominates the smallness of clustered humans and represents human inferiority to the divine. Each figure exhibits a separate personality with the exception of the humans, who are almost identical. The horizontal bands and variations in scale are said to stop the viewer's eyes from wandering and concentrate attention on the meaning of each layer. Totem eyes peer out in various directions, and there is less rigidity in the carvings than the strict discipline apparent in traditional Kwakiutl poles.

A second unique feature of some of Tsimshian poles is their simplicity. Certain poles (not shown here) are no more than a long unornamented shaft surmounted by one three-dimensional animal. This type of pole provides a contrast to the heavily ornamented surrounding poles and serves to elevate the eye up to the crowning figure. An example of this type of pole is shown on page 19.

Traditional Tsimshian poles are largely monuments erected by various families to commemorate their chiefs after death. They correspond roughly to tombstones. Scholars surmise that it was the Tsimshian peoples along the Nass and Skeena Rivers who

Nuxälk-style

Kwakiutl-style

Tsimshian-style

created the first clusters of free standing totem poles.

Haida-style poles reflect their people, who were a seafaring lot and regularly visited their neighbours to the north and south. This and their excellence in the arts explains the wide influence that the Haida style continues to exert on the totem pole tradition of the Northwest Coast. Shown here is a tall Haida pole cut into three pieces to illustrate the characteristic "eye set" of the figures. Far from a vacant stare, Haida eyes are designed to peer down at the viewer from their position on the pole. Well-formed eyes feature inner pupils and outer lids, pinched on two sides. The figures peer down in eternal watchfulness. The higher the figure on the pole, the more angled downward its gaze. Haida poles are typically unpainted and feature voluptuously carved semi-human and animal figures. The lines of Haida poles flow from one decoration to the next. Humans, if they appear at all, are smaller than other figures. Some feature a thrusting tongue. Thun-

derbird does not feature in their depictions. All Haida poles show fully dimensioned animals, with well-rounded body parts and separate personalities.

In times past, Haida poles were mainly monuments erected by various families to commemorate important people after death or to commemorate the happenings at a potlatch.

Coast Salish–style poles were uncommon. The Coast Salish people and their cousins to the south traditionally did not build totem poles or create multitudes of different masks. While many band members have adapted to new ways and now build impressive freestanding poles, the characteristic carvings of these people were single figures. These wooden human figures adorned graves or stood along the shoreline to attract the attention of their seafaring neighbours. Today, called greet figures or welcome figures, the traditions behind these slightly-larger-than-life-sized "poles" go further back than the carving of regular tall totem poles. Coast Salish people today do carve de-

tached totem poles. Some appear to be a number of greet figures, one on top of the next; others look like an amalgam of several tribal and artistic styles.

Nuxälk-style pole art is not well known and exerts a minor influence on modern traditions. Isolated in a deep mountain valley, the Nuxälk (Bella Coola) people once had few visitors and thus developed their own unique style. Relative latecomers to the art of totem pole construction, Nuxälk poles feature well defined and separated shapes such as teardrop, triangle, and leaf shapes, slightly uncharacteristic of other Northwest Coast traditions. The poles are brightly painted and have few add-ons. Eyes stare straight ahead and contain a contrasting coloured pupil.

Today, the Nuxälk are renowned in artistic circles for depicting the round-faced figure of Siskiutl in a deep blue colour to match the skies and ocean of their homeland. Their execution of this creature surpasses that of all other traditions. A Nuxälk Siskiutl is pictured on page 87.

times carries a basket to capture small children. As a masked dance figure, Dzunkwa holds her hands palm out in front of her mouth and eyes, in order to hide her true intents. In certain stories, it is said her hands are sharp as knives. On public totem poles she sometimes stands, arms open, attracting hoards of unsuspecting tourists into her wide embrace.

Mosquito has a long proboscis and is sometimes mistaken for a bird. But his crafty eyes give his true tastes away. He is a story figure, not a heraldic crest.

Dzunkwa's Personality and Habits

Dzunkwa is an uncivilized, brutish woman who lives in the forest. Suffering from some sort of sleeping (or drug-induced) disorder, she sleeps much. Her eyes are slit-like, and even when awake she is trance-like in her movements. In her active periods, she prowls the edge of villages attempting to satisfy her appetite for children's flesh. Sometimes she has to settle for stealing fish. Her house is made from fir branches, and when awake she gathers roots, flowers, herbs, and resins from which she concocts a tasty gum-confection to attract children and glue their eyes shut. Always saccharin in her approach, her true intents are murderous.

In recent times, political correctness has unfortunately edited her pendulous breasts and her personality. In one case she was recently described by a major museum as a "loving mother embracing the world." Dzunkwa would be pleased. She has several chil-

The Goodwill Pole

"GOODWILL" HAS MANY shades of meaning but rarely rises to the ironic levels of the Goodwill Pole. In 1899, a Goodwill Mission travelled to Tongass, Alaska, to "help" the natives. During their stay, the visitors pilfered a pole and removed it to Seattle. The villagers immediately sent representatives south to protest—to no avail. In 1941, as part of the first serious efforts to preserve US totem poles, descendants of the Tongass villagers were employed to restore the totem pole in Pioneer Square. As a gesture of "goodwill," they officially presented it to the city of Seattle.

Ainu Poles

THE AINU, the aboriginal people of northern Japan's Hokkaido island, also carve poles. Ainu mythology tells of a people closely connected to water. Pole groupings such as these represent the "Playground of the Gods" and tell the story of supernatural beings who came to earth to give birth to them. Bear, Owl, and Orca are particularly significant figures for they are the earthly disguises the gods assume. Ainu pole groupings are designed to complement the background scenery. Each pole is simply made and it is the sum

of the grouping that creates the effect.

Frog is associated with granting wealth

Frog

Frog is the heraldic crest of several active clan lineages that exist to the present day. In Western cultures, Frog usually belongs to the beast-marriage cycle as in *The Frog Prince*, or *Frog Went a-Courting.* Along the Northwest Coast, Frog never appears in marriage sagas; Instead, Frog plays a peripheral role in stories and in one tale (not related here), each time a frog is sighted, a voice cries out for the return of a beloved daughter who has died.

The qualities admired in Frog are its abilities to survive red hot volcanic lava flows or scorching fires, to live on land or in water with equal aplomb, and to burrow deep in mud yet continue to breathe. Frog has several alternate personas and in those forms is associated with bringing copper and wealth up to the surface from underwater cities.

Frog's Appearance

Very realistic in interpretation, Frogs appear top to bottom, or bottom to top, hidden in other figures' ears, on top of their heads, or embedded in their belly buttons. In each case, Frog represents the Frog clan's association with the pole.

Frog's Personality and Habits

Little is related about Frog except for its usual shift-shaping qualities and its occasional transformation relationship with Copper Woman and Woman of Fire.

Frog's Powers

In one story, Frogs are associated with calling humans who come back from apparent death, but exactly what power

dren of her own. What exact psychological problems they exhibit are not fully explored. Since they are taboo, she does not eat them. In fact, she is deeply upset when they are injured, maimed, killed, or spirited away and put on display. She makes heroic efforts to resurrect them. The attack on her children is unrelenting. Anyone who can make her babies cry can demand her treasures. These include a magic canoe, water of life, or death-bringer (handy if you are really angry at someone). Compassionate humans, who help her get her children back, are showered with gifts.

Bookwus, on the other hand, engages in slightly fewer forays for human prey and prefers to fraternize with frightening ghosts.

Dzunkwa's Powers

Significant among Dzunkwa's power is her ability to resurrect herself from the dead. Even with her brains smashed out and her body dismembered, she can reassemble and come alive. She also can use this power with her own children, who have frequently been murdered to spite her. If she can get their bodies back, she can rouse them from the dead.

Dzunkwa's Relationship with Humans

Sometimes, Dzunkwa leaves her home in the forest and visits humans during their Winter Dances. When inside the longhouse, a human attendant ropes her around the waist with a leash. Because she is permanently dazed and in some sort of hypnotic state, unless she has help, she cannot circle the fire four times before she falls in. Those fortunate enough to come across Dzunkwa's home while she is away come back with dried meats, skins, statues, and coppers. She enjoys a lively side-practice of thievery and has been known to pilfer a hunter's or fisher's entire catch. Her greatest interest in humans, however, is dietary.

Frog brings to bear on this process is not quite clear. In another story, Frog is held down in a fire with a stick and when it bursts, a lava flow engulfs the village. Copper Woman, Frog's transformed self, associate, or alter ego, is noted for bringing wealth. She is the wife of Komokwa, or Copper Maker, a powerful guardian of the undersea world. Woman of Fire, Frog's second persona, is noted for her destructive tendencies.

Frog's Relationship with Humans

Frogs are generally unconcerned about humans and in many instances are treated with contempt. In one story, a fisher and his companions prepare their catch over an evening campfire. From out of the darkness, a Frog leaps out and pushes their dinner into the flames. The vexed humans kill the creature and begin to cook their dinner over again. A larger Frog, with bright copper eyes, hops out and repeats the action. The angry humans burn it. The third time, a larger-than-life Woman appears in a pillar of flame. In her hand, she carries a talking stick mounted with a copper Frog. She tells the fisher that he and his companions will die. After many other story incidents, related one by one, all happens as foretold.

Human Forms and Human Objects

Coppers are shield-shaped devices that played an important role during a potlatch. On totem poles, a copper often means that the owner of the pole is displaying a heraldic animal or figure for the first time.

Frog is the heraldic crest of the Frog clan

The right or prerogative to carve an animal or heraldic figure was granted to the pole's owner in one of three ways:

    (a) at a potlatch
    (b) through war
    (c) through an encounter with a supernatural figure

    To show that the new prerogative is approved , the new animal or figure holds a copper. A Bear with copper appears on page 35.

Chiefs

Chiefs are recognized by their three-ringed hats. Each time an elder was able to mount a pot-

A Frog Story

IN THE TIME before this, a great man climbed a high mountain to learn what he could from Mountain-Spirit. While on top, he had a vision. A Giant Frog came and told him that humans and frogs were part of the oneness of all. Humans should treat Frog with more respect. When the man came out of his trance and returned to his people, they took Frog as their emblem and built totem crests in honour of Frog.

Humans

Humans clustered in horizontal bands on Tsimshian poles represent the lesser role of helpless humans as contrasted with the superior powers of transforming animals and mythological beings. On modern poles, it has become fashionable to show humans joining hands to illustrate a spirit of cooperation among all of humanity.

White people, such as the man in a top hat crowning the famous Abraham Lincoln pole in Alaska, represent the coming of Europeans to liberate or dominate native cultures. The Lincoln figure, now kept indoors at a museum in Juneau, Alaska, was erected in Tongas village about 1870 to proclaim that President Abraham Lincoln had liberated Native American people as well as southern slaves.

Mountain Goat

Mountain Goat is part of the cycle of stories about redressing the imbalance caused by hunters. It is also a heraldic crest. A fairly rare depiction on totem poles, its heraldic variations are Painted Mountain Goat and Mountain Goat of Skedans. The Raven phratry has rights to display Mountain Goat.

Mountain Goat's Appearance

With one or two prominent horns and hoofed feet, Mountain Goat is occasionally mistaken for some sort of a devil depiction. This is not the case. Its hooves and horns simply reflect its natural ungulate form.

Crying Woman

latch, he was entitled to weave another ring on top of his cedar-strip hat. Three seems to be the maximum number shown on poles, although hats with up to seven rings are displayed in some museums. A chief's presence on a pole usually means he commissioned the totem pole. His carvers have wisely chosen to feature the image of their benefactor among the heraldic crests and story figures.

Clusters of three chiefs represent the Haida Watchmen, an ancient society entrusted with guarding Haida Gwaii, the ancestral home of the Haida nation

Crying Woman

Crying Woman is a story figure, not a heraldic crest, on several poles. In each of her appearances, she is crying for a different reason. On one famous pole near the Skeena river, she is crying because she has captured a grouse to save her starving son, but she is too late.

A Composite of Raven Stories

THE FOLLOWING RAVEN story is not a children's fable and is not suitable for children. This condensation is derived from written recordings of some of the scores of stories up to a century old. Raven is part of the very important story of the origin of First People and is interwoven with their identity. Children's versions of Raven stories are edited for content.

"Raven was going along" are the translated native words commencing all Raven trickster stories.

In the time before this, a woman was crying because all her children were stillborn. By and by, Heron came to her and advised her to go to the beach, find a smooth stone, and place it into a fire. When it was hot and blackened, she was instructed to swallow it. She followed Heron's directions and later gave birth to Raven. That is why Raven is so black and tough.

Raven was going along, a difficult child, always attracting disasters. A tree fell on him; a canoe snapped shut on him; he fell into a fire pit; he was boiled in a kettle. Using his supernatural powers, he survived all of these incidents. For the act of seducing his aunt (or in other stories, the daughter of the Sky-Chief), the world was deluged. He heroically rescued his mother

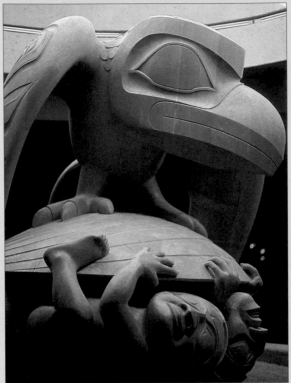

from the flood, then nonchalantly flew away in his bird form. During adolescence, his appetite became so voracious he ate the spots off his toes. He began to wander in search of things to eat and situations to keep himself amused. The world at that time was without a sun, being only dimly lit by an unnamed light source, inhabited by a few semi-humans, and mostly devoid of life.

Raven was going along when he encountered a bighouse where he discovered a chief who kept several valuable treasures locked up in a series of nested boxes. Unable to trick the chief into letting him enter the house, he turned himself into a speck of dirt and by way of a

drop of water, the chief's attractive daughter swallowed him. When her time was completed, he was born to the young woman and masqueraded as a fast-growing human child. Living inside the house and enjoying his mother's nurturing, he was an exasperating, hyperactive toddler. Making a great fuss and whining for the nested boxes, his wishes were finally granted. One by one, he liberated the sun, the moon, and the stars, all secured in the boxes. The heavenly bodies streaked upward through the smoke hole and came to rest in the sky as we know them today. Thus satisfied, he casually resumed his form as Raven.

Leaving this place, Raven was going along when he came to the shore. There some creatures had secretly made a fire. Stealing a flaming branch, but not exactly knowing what it was, he accidentally set himself ablaze and burned off part of his beak. That is why Ravens are blackened and have short beaks.

Raven was going along having many other adventures. He stuck spiny sea urchins onto an old woman's buttocks and stopped only when she promised to regulate the tides. He tricked the man who controls fresh water via the use of dog excrement in a messy adventure. He went to war with South Wind to bring good weather. Raven was responsible for all the fish in the water. He forced Gull to spit up oolichans, which continued to propagate in the sea. Raven is credited with releasing the first Salmon too. Later he married, then betrayed, a spirit-wife who was skillful at catching and preserving salmon. He emasculated a Grizzly Bear during a friendly fishing trip. He tore out Cormorant's tongue. He played dead and was buried so he could resurrect himself and marry his daughter. He was swallowed by Whale. He also had adven-

tures as a human woman. All these adventures resulted in the liberating of a vital component onto the earth.

Resting for a while, Raven became bored. One day, Raven was going along searching the sandy beaches when his attention was distracted by several little creatures squirming inside a giant clamshell. Liberating them from their shell-cage, he watched with amusement as the tiny, naked, male human-like figures played in the sand. A crafty idea stole over him. Picking the figures up in his beak, he took them to a nearby tidal pool

where there were thousands of soft, fleshy sea-mollusks clinging to the rocks. Much to Raven's amusement, the little men "fraternized" with the mollusks, who immediately began to swell. The mollusks later increased to an enormous size and gave birth to full-sized humans. That is how Raven liberated or "created" human beings as they are known today.

Raven had many other adventures. His thievery included stealing salmon eggs, his sister's berries, and various shiny objects. As a dinner

host who tries to produce food magically, he bungled it. As a friend of Deer, he killed his companion. Finally, human beings caught onto his deceptive ways, and Raven himself was captured, tortured, cut up, and murdered. In each of these adventures, he reconstituted himself. And that is how Raven was going along and how he always is.

Mountain Goat's Personality and Habits

Living in active community houses with social rights and relatives, Mountain Goats are noted for their great feasts and excellent culinary skills. Even when shifted into human form, they like to include grass in their diet.

Mountain Goat's Powers

With all the regular transformational qualities of other animals, Mountain Goat can easily take on the form of a human. Kids tend to manifest as human children. Mountain Goats also have the power to cause massive rock slides.

Mountain Goat's Relationship with Humans

Generally tending to avoid humans and take little notice of them, Mountain Goats are capable of planned revenge when injustices are committed.

Raven

Raven is a figure of both honour and derision among Native people. In several North American native mythologies, the creation of the earth and humanity are not attributed to a

Raven is a symbol of honour

supreme being, but to an agent of that power. The details of creation are left to a subordinate type of deity. This subcreator actually causes and organizes the details of the world and has the personality and powers of a hero-trickster-transformer. Among Northwest Coast Natives that figure is generally depicted as Raven.

Ravens and crows are confused with each other in most of the world and that fact is of no great consequence to these stories. The European predilection to associate ravens with

bad-omens, pestilence, and death, however, is not generally shared by aboriginal cultures. Instead, Raven's creative and trickster abilities are celebrated around the world. The Malays, the Australian Aborigines, the Vietnamese, and the Ainu of Japan share Raven stories remarkably similar to those of the Northwest Coast. As far away as eastern Siberia, Bear stories have a strong resemblance to Raven adventures. In South American native cultures, a trickster Fox takes absurd initiatives.

A Siskiutl Story

IN THE TIME BEFORE this one, Thunderbird and his wife shifted shapes and came to this world to take in the Winter Dances and to begin their own tribe. Appearing as humans, they were known as Head-Winter-Dancer and Winter-Dance-Woman. Just as celebrations began, the wife gave birth to their fourth son. About the same time, Head-Winter-Dancer caught a strange-looking salmon in his trap. In vain he tried to club it, but it became wilder and wilder. Remembering the advice

of his wife, he bit his own tongue and spit blood on it. As the fish calmed, he knew he had killed a transformed Siskiutl. Bringing back the gift, he knew his wife would be pleased for the sea serpent brought great powers to warriors. Cutting the serpent in half, his wife bathed their baby son in its blood. Instantly, the child became twice the size of a full-grown man and appeared to be made of stone. His face resembled Dzunkwa, the Wild-Woman. His parents were

thrilled.

Immediately, the son set out to make war all over the world. (The attendant rituals form a part of the story, but they are not related here.) The boy received a special death-bringing canoe that was formed from impervious wood and sported a serpent's head at each end. Self-propelled and self-navigating, the canoe paddled only on its owner's command. With these powers, the son brought back wealth, prerogatives, and slaves for his family.

Opposite: Siskiutl

The Raven cycle of stories are the most important tales along the Northwest Coast. Raven-as-bird aptly fills the role of transformer among northern people, though his persona, powers, and attributes are occasionally switched to the characters Mink (or Kwati) on Vancouver Island and to Bluejay farther south. In the interior and Okanagan region, Coyote and his friend Wolf exhibit all Raven's trickster qualities but have fewer of his appetites and powers. However Raven himself is the greatest transformer-trickster of all.

Raven is the chief character in a series of Northwest Coast tales including *The Birth of Raven, Raven and the Creation of Humans, Raven Liberates Light, Raven Steals Fire, Raven is Swallowed By Whale,* and *Raven Kills Deer.* In 1916, Franz Boas, an ethnographer, listed 45 principal Raven stories from earlier times, but notes that the tales were even more numerous.

The fact that a creator figure can be altruistic, heroic, and creative one moment, then grotesque and greedy the next, is sometimes puzzling to outsiders. Transformer traditions do not recognize the difference between the secular and the profane.

"Thank you, Swimmers, you Supernatural Ones, that you have come to save our lives….Do not feel wrong about what I have done to you, friend Swimmer, that is the reason why you came, that I may spear you, that I may eat you…"
—*Various groups, Chant to Salmon*

Raven's Appearance

A large, omnivorous bird resembling a crow, Raven has a long, heavy-looking beak with a slight curve that can thrust out or be integrated downward into his design. Sometimes he holds Sun or Moon in his mouth.

Raven's Personality and Habits

Raven is restless, curious and to an intense degree, easily bored, always looking for exciting adventures. His voracious appetites for both food and sexual delights are legendary and cause many of his troubles. Unlike other trickster figures (such as Coyote, who is always seen in league with Wolf), Raven is a loner. He exhibits no guilt or remorse, even for the act of murder. Practical jokes are a part of Native life, and Raven embodies the restless necessity to avoid rules and keep oneself entertained— even at the expense of others.

In his elevated form, Raven plays the role of creator: changing the landscape; liberating the sun, moon, and stars; and making over each animal in their present-day form. As a hero, Raven is responsible for cultural innovations such as teaching humans how to use fire. As a deceiving trickster, however, he is a liar, a thief, a cheat, a pervert, and a murderer. He can be selfish and childlike. He can also be a seducer of some skill or an innovative fop. Sometimes deceptively clever, at other times he is plain stupid.

Raven's Powers

Raven's greatest powers cluster around transformation and shape-shifting on his own or causing it in others. Not only can he become any human or animal, he can take on the shape of a twig, leaf, stone, or any object. Unlike other transformers, he has an uncanny ability to exactly duplicate the qualities of his subject. For example, when Bear becomes human, it retains a lumbering, slow, bear-like personality. Not so, Raven. His transformation is complete to the last detail. He can also be swallowed (as a pine needle, for example) and through that route causes a woman to give birth. She then delivers a human form (Raven) who grows quickly. He usually (but not always) resumes his black bird form after taking a human wife.

Raven also owns a cloak of invisibility, but seems less powerful in that form. Occasionally his transformation powers are so perfect, he has a bit of trouble reconstituting his bird form. In one story, in his transformed character, he is cut up and thrown down a latrine hole. In that position, he has some difficulty pulling himself together and spends days at the bottom of an in-service pit.

Raven's Relationship with Humans

Raven has two patterns of relationship with humans. In one he is revered, and held in formal esteem as the supreme being's agent in creation. This honour he receives during the raising of a totem pole or the honouring of a dead chief. In his less serious role, he is simply considered an amusing fop to be laughed at.

Raven has the power to transform

Raven has many names, ranging from He Whose Voice Is Obeyed to Greedy One. Humans in the past have occasionally become annoyed with the trickster side of his personality and have burned, tortured, murdered, and mutilated him. He regenerates with varying degrees of difficulty. Among the Kwakiutl people, Raven has an additional incarnation as Kwakwakwalanooksiwae, the raven by the water, who is the instigator of three manifestations of Cannibal Bird.

His life seems to have one outstanding quality to it. Whatever adventures Raven indulges in become part of the reality of human existence forevermore.

Salmon and Other Fish

Salmon-eaters, Salmon, and other fish are somewhat rare depictions on totem poles. The tradition of the Salmon-eater clan among the Tsimshian and others embodies what the Natives of three northern Pacific nations consider the true story of their migrations out of the foam of the sea. Many Native people are reluctant to believe in anthropologists' theory of the land-bridge between Asia and North America. The Salmon-eater cycle of stories is thought to echo the migrations of the people, from Alaska to

The Cedar Tree

KNOWN VARIOUSLY AS the canoe cedar, giant cedar, western red cedar, shinglewood, or arbor-vitae, the *Thuja plicata* grows in the rainforests of the Northwest Coast. Its wood is soft, relatively light in weight, and easy to split. Its cinnamon-red or greyish brown bark is stringy and fibrous, making it easy to weave, plait, or roll into ropes. A second species called yellow cedar, Alaska cedar, Nootka cypress, or Sitka cypress, the *Chamaecyparis nootkatensis* resembles red cedar in its qualities but has a satin-like, light, creamy yellow wood.

Here, Bear holds a flat flounder. Note its two eyes. Today, carvers increasingly show Bear with Salmon.

catching them. Salmon are, at most, personified story characters with vital regenerative powers.

Salmon's Appearance

In previous times, Salmon appeared incidentally, as objects in Bear's hands or among a Whale's fins. They are shaped like their natural counterpart. Recent depictions of Salmon have elevated them to a higher level. At the insistence of non-Native patrons of the arts, several modern murals and paintings glorify Salmon's contributions to its people.

Salmon's Personality and Habits

Salmon are fairly docile beings and have no problem offering themselves as food to humans. Their extraordinary regenerative abilities keep them from remaining dead—as long as humans observe certain rituals such as disposing properly of every morsel and bone.

Salmon's Powers

Salmon live in underwater villages, speak in their own tongues, and deliberately set out from their homes to sacrifice themselves for the benefit of humans. First Salmon Caught is the most important. Once captured, a special ceremony is held. Chiefs, dressed in full regalia, sprinkle red ochre on its body. Songs are sung and Salmon is placed on a cedar mat and paraded in honour among the people. It is cut with a ritual knife and a tiny piece given to each of the fishing families. Its bones are carefully saved and returned to the water. In this way, the bones reconstitute, and Salmon returns to let its own kind know of their honour among humans.

the places where they eventually settled up to the point of European contact. There is not room in this text to relate these long, involved, and symbolic stories here. Salmon-eaters along the Nass branched out into several other phratries, and the clan's origins are bound up in a long story about sinful people destroyed by a volcanic eruption. The Wolf phratry has the right to display Salmon-eater figures.

One particularly powerful house crest among the Haida is Dogfish Woman, a powerful

creature who appears in rare depictions. She is discreetly naked but sports a crown, appearing more as a queen than a bottom-dwelling fish. She is related to Shark, who also plays a role in Haida stories. Other fish creatures playing a minor role on some totem poles are Codfish and Cod Woman.

As fish, salmon are of middling importance in the traditional stories of the Northwest Coast. Since salmon are the main food, it would hardly be an honour to be descended from them. The honour is in

Salmon's Relationship with Humans

People sometimes travel to underwater Salmon villages and cities. Humans have no trouble breathing and seeing Salmon in human form. The greatest problem is sharing a meal. Salmon people do not eat salmon. When a human visitor is hungry, he bonks a village child on the head. The child immediately turns into a fish and the visitor eats it. Placing the fish bones carefully back into the water, the visitor goes to bed. The child is seen playing happily the next day.

In one Haida story, a boy disappears. One day his father catches an enormous Salmon. The son is gradually discovered by his mother as she cuts it open. He has been turned into Salmon. His parents use rituals and herbs to shift his shape back to human form.

Siskiutl

Sea Monster, or Siskiutl, a two-headed sea snake representing "strength among warriors," is a common heraldic crest among several coastal nations. It is either Siskiutl's brother or a land-based incarnation who is known to the Tlingit people as Giant Woodworm. There are many Siskiutls and Woodworms in the world.

An encounter with Siskiutl is dangerous to all but its heraldic crest holders. These kinsfolk own specific bits of its body said to bestow great powers. For example, the warrior Winaxwinagam owned a Siskiutl spine-knife. It could cut through anything and could not be taken away from him. When he was captured, his enemies cut slits through his thighs and back and hung him upside down from the rafters. Swinging his knife wildly, the warrior was unable to reach his bonds. However, the cuts he inflicted on himself turned out to be a pleasurable experience. Contradictions, such as being calmed at the sight of blood, are associated with Siskiutl.

Siskiutl's clanswomen have the ability to perform dances and wave magic wands to coax the creatures from their lairs. Small Siskiutls arrive on wing and larger ones poke their horns up from trenches connected to the underworld.

Its long slender shape makes Siskiutl particularly popular as a design for belts, headbands, talking sticks, and as bow decorations. On totem

> *Welcome, Great Chief, Father, as you come and show yourself this morning. We come and meet. Alive.*
> —*Kwakiutl, Chant to the Sun at Sunrise*

Whale

Siskiutl's Powers

Said to live comfortably in a form as small as an insect grub, Siskiutl can exist on the land or under the sea. At will it can increase to the enormous size of a sea serpent. Naturally able to speak human tongues, its two heads often think in contradictions. When in a helpful mood, it turns into a self-navigating, self-paddling canoe. In this form it can deliver a war party to the enemy's shores. Other times, however, it has been known to eat canoes, people and all.

When living on land as Woodworm, its voracious appetite is the flaw that ultimately results in the whole village taking up arms against it. In another of its shape shiftings, it appears as an ordinary salmon.

To see, eat, or touch Siskiutl is said to be unlucky and might cause death. Some report that one long glare from Siskiutl can twist human joints round into a permanent backwards position. However, this is by no means a certain fate, as several of its crest holders are known to have killed a specimen and obtained portions of its body. To possess a piece, especially the skin, scales, spines, or blood, brings good fortune in fishing, in fighting, and in life. Siskiutl blood is particularly poisonous. However, those who know its secrets can partake of its great powers. When properly applied to arrow tips, it petrifies the enemy on contact. When rubbed on a warrior's body the blood makes him impervious to injury.

Siskiutl owns a sling used in battles with its enemy, the Thunderbird. Human warriors

Two headed Siskiutl appears under Sun

poles, the viewer must travel all the way round the pole to see its two or three heads.

Siskiutl's Appearance

Siskiutl has a jolly, roundish face and a cylindrical body that terminates at each end with a serpent's head. All three faces sport curly horn-like protuberances and the two end-heads feature darting red tongues. Among the Nuxälk (Bella Coola) people, its middle face is coloured a deep periwinkle blue. In the ocean, Siskiutl has iridescent scales and moves with the help of fins or swim-legs, somewhat invisible to humans.

Siskiutl's Personality and Habits

Siskiutl's outstanding trait seems to be its ambiguous nature—sometimes a death-dealing monster and sometimes a helpful bestower of good fortune. Only the holders of its clan rights can be certain of its

In some stories Sun is carried across the sky each day by an old grandmother

once borrowed this weapon, using Siskiutl eyes as projectiles. The enemy turned to stone. Occasionally this event is signified by a quartz crystal embedded in Siskiutl's forehead.

In some cases, the image of Siskiutl alone is enough to vanquish an enemy. In one instance Mink triumphed over rival Wolf, by using a Siskiutl mask. Human warriors sometimes wear Siskiutl belts carefully hidden under their outer clothing. One direct look at a properly empowered belt can knock an enemy instantly dead.

Siskiutl's Relationship with Humans

Being naturally powerful, Siskiutl occasionally lends its kinsfolk a helping hand; others experience its destructive nature. In modern times, some say Siskiutl represents the fact that good luck comes with an equal and opposite propensity for bad luck. For example, if a person wins the lottery, a close friend might die.

left: Bear

Sun and Moon

Sun and Moon are heavenly bodies that have always held particular fascination for tribes located in hot desert or dry plains areas. The image of Sun enjoys a strong personification among the Plains, Southwest, Natchez, and Yuchi tribes. Among the Inuit, Iroquois, Cherokee, and Ojibwa, Sun and Moon both hold an honoured place. None outdo the Sun cult and its symbols among Central and South American Aztec and Inca groups.

In the rainy Northwest Coast, both Sun and Moon are accorded strong totemic images, but they play an insignificant role in stories. In Kwakiutl stories, the figure Mink is sometimes referred to as Son of the Sunshine. The Nuxälk people hold Sun and Moon in the greatest accord. In their Sisauk Dance society, these beings, along with Echo and Earthquake, play an important role. Other than these exceptions, Sun and Moon hold marginal positions in Northwest Coast native stories.

Many North American native languages have no specific word for "moon" and "sun." These heavenly bodies are specified with the same words as "daylight" and "nighttime". Also, there is no universal agreement on the gender of heavenly bodies. Unlike Western convention, Sun might be female and Moon a male figure. The Chehalis people of present-day state of Washington feature Moon as their changer-creator-transformer figure and consider it male, whereas the Tillamook people present Moon as a female changer.

Usually portrayed as a circle with a full face, a hawk-like beak, and protruding beams, Sun lacks a warm smile but does have an animated visage. Moon is portrayed as a round circle with a male-human face and no protruding rays. Occasionally the crescent moon is painted inside the circle. Neither are noted for talking or having a relationship with humans. Their powers, though extraordinary, remain relatively undefined among Northwest Coast native cultures.

Whales

Whales, Whale-Killer, Killer Whale, Double-Finned Whale, and Fin of Killer Whale are crests among the Tlingit, among the Nisga'a, along the Nass River, and among the Haida. Whales are honoured as strong and brave fish (yes, fish) who, in the stories, first materialized or transformed out of three cedar sculptures carved in their likeness. In this form, they brought food or assistance to a chief or important person lying helpless and wounded by

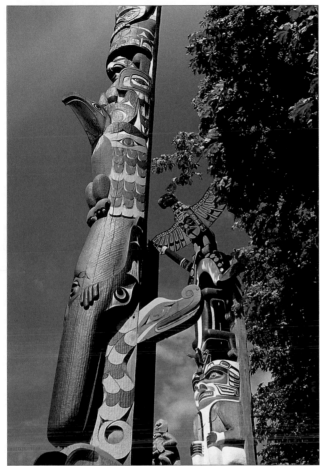

Whale appears beside one head of Siskiutl. Thunderbird conquers another Whale behind.

crest related to this practice is the powerful Sea Wolf or Wasco image; some say it is not Wolf at all but a powerful Grizzly-Bear-of-the-Sea. Wasco (in Wolf form) hunts whales and lives in a mountain lake near Skidegate.

A whale carcass or two usually floated ashore each year and its meat was greatly savoured by the tribes that did not venture onto the open seas to hunt whales. It is said that because a cedar-made Whale figure once carried out the wishes of a starving human, whale fat crackles in the fire just like wood.

Whale's Appearance

Two species of whales can be distinguished on totem poles: Gray Whales and Killer Whales. Their body parts are sometimes rearranged with the tail, major fins, and head appearing in a somewhat detached fashion, fitting as necessary around the pole. On several poles, the dorsal fin is attached as a separate piece and thus is subject to falling off. Whale is usually carved head down, and on many totem poles happy faces peak out from the blow hole. There is no significance to these happy figures; Native carvers simply like to fill spaces with interesting designs.

Whale's Personality and Habits

Whale is generally seen as prey so its personality and habits, powers, and relationship with humans, like Salmon, are less defined than some of the greater entities. It is difficult to include likable personalities on the menu. In the Thunderbird story, one particularly obnoxious giant Whale plays a major role as the antagonist. In other

an arrow. Whale then went to live, with many personified sea creatures, in an underwater city. This act of kindness granted the descendants of the injured person the right to use Whale's crest.

Since ancient times, harpooning whales at the climax of fortnight-long seagoing voyages was the activity of the Nootka people. Because of the dangers involved, great ceremonies verging on shamanism were part of the practice. Whaling team members were initi-

left: Wolf

ated, underwent fasts, were ritually prepared, watched special dances, and enjoyed rights greater than ordinary individuals. Whale as a totem figure on some poles descends from the rights of whalers and whaling.

Among the Kwakiutl and others, it was said that Whale came ashore after a long time at sea, plowed up on the land, and changed into Wolf. In that shape, it enjoyed hunting land animals and occasionally its own kind. In Wolf form, it revealed the secrets of the Whale cult to all humans. The Haida

IN THE TIME BEFORE this, there was a great famine upon the land. Now the people were starving. Their discomfort was heightened night after night as they listened to the beating of drums and loud howling songs coming from across the river. The people were afraid to go out, even in daylight.

One brave warrior volunteered to investigate. Venturing forth in his ceremonial robes, his face painted, his long hair tied in a knot, and armed with weapons, he ventured out. (These rituals form a part of the story, but they are not related here.)

Crossing the river he came upon a huge Wolf, whining in agony. As the warrior approached, it laid back its ears and gazed at the intruder, begging with pathetic eyes. "Come brother, what has happened?" the warrior inquired. Wolf could not speak, but opened its mouth in a cavernous yawn. Sizing up the situation, the warrior approached. Behold, a deer bone was stuck in Wolf's throat.

With reassuring words, the warrior removed the bone and Wolf immediately recovered. Joyously, it licked the warrior's hands and feet. Then emitting a loud howl, it disappeared into the forest.

The next day there was a tumultuous howling from across the river and the people could see scores of Wolves pacing restlessly on the opposite shore. The warrior and his companions were once again summoned. While the party was crossing the river, the Wolves disappeared. Arranged along the opposite bank lay sev-

eral deer carcasses. There was great rejoicing among the hungry people. Each day more deer carcasses appeared, along with mink, martin, and groundhog to be distributed as gifts. The warrior and his people were able to mount great feasts. By the prerogative of this event, all these people adopted the Wolf crest. It is said by some that the warrior himself was made Prince-of-the-Wolves.

The story goes on to explain how their association with Wolf permitted them to obtain magical headdresses and robes from the Ghost-People. (These rituals may

form a significant part of the story, but they are not related here.)

Sometime after, strife broke out and there were disputes over who had abused certain privileges associated with the masks taken from the Ghost-People. In the end, the warrior and his immediate family left their tribe and went to a new area to found a new Wolf phratry. Other branches of Wolf clan use the heralds Tall Conical Hat, Long Sharp Nose, Hanging Across Half Man, and Sea-Wolf. Wolf phratries once claimed the rights to the tallest poles along the Nass River.

stories, Whales are well known to be the prey of Thunderbird and Eagle.

Wolf

Wolf has a varied reputation throughout the world. Its faithfulness to its family and strong group loyalties have done little to prevent it being maligned by many societies. Being associated with evil, it was hunted to extinction in much of Europe.

Among North American native people, Wolf exhibits a nobler personality. Wolf and Raven, or Wolf and Beaver are moiety divisions of the Tlingit people. Wolf is also prominent in the heraldic imagery of Coast Salish, Quileute, and Makah (southern Nootka) peoples.

Some of the first "human" Wolf phratries claim blood relationship to the animal. It seems four cubs survived a great flood by climbing to the top of a tall mountain. There, they removed their clothing and became human. Eventually, their offspring wondered if they were the only people in the world. Putting on Wolf masks, they howled aloud. Finally their cries were met with an answer. They left the mountain and went to live among ordinary humans. There are several variations of this story. Other Wolf clan origin stories are taken from the cycle of "grateful animal" tales.

Wolf's Appearance

Wolves have long muzzles with sharp teeth, but usually not the sharp incisor teeth of Bear. Bear also has a shorter muzzle and more rounded nostrils. Wolf's ears are pointed. Wolf can be integrated on a pole from top to bottom or in full body sitting on its haunches. The tail is sometimes present and sometimes not. In recent depictions, Wolf looks quite realistic.

Wolf's Personality and Habits

Wolves live in remotely located communities, in enormous bighouses, and have all the normal feelings associated with families toward their brothers, sisters, children, and spouses. Stories do not say whether they keep slaves. Deer are their favourite prey. Though Wolves know the secrets of hunting and curing sickness, they are little inclined to share either with humans.

Wolf's Powers

Taking on the form of humans and speaking in human tongues are basic animal powers. In the case of Wolf though, transformational powers sometimes occur in reverse. Certain humans not only become like Wolf, they become Wolf.

Wolf packs host elaborate late-night dance celebrations noted for loud drumming, howling songs, and beautiful women. During these ceremonials, Wolves transform into lively human-looking dancers and are known to fraternize with long-dead Ghost-People. Occasionally, humans have crept unnoticed into these ceremonies, only realizing their folly when they play a trick on a female dancer: trying to reach up a dancer's skirts, they feel nothing but the bare bones of death.

Wolf will sometimes travel to the ocean and change into Whale. This is why both wolves and killer whales hunt in packs.

Wolf's Relationship with Humans

Mostly wary of human encounters, Wolf nevertheless retains the ability to commit to friendships and render helpful services to people. According to some, a Wolf (transformed from Whale) once revealed the secrets of hunting Whale. Usually, however, Wolves show a vague lack of interest in human affairs, preferring the camaraderie of their own kind. One Wolf society originated when a great shaman killed a Wolf chief and danced in his skin, thereby gaining the power to cure all ailments. Wolf society members know many secrets; certain members can even become Wolf. This society will enact the Wolf dance for a sick person, but the charge for such a cure is very high.

Traditional Cedar Products

THESE ARE SOME traditional cedar products made by the First Nations people:
- large canoes
- nets, traps, weirs, and harpoons to harvest salmon
- watertight bentwood boxes for cooking
- storage boxes
- large plankhouses to house up to 50 families
- cedar bark mats used for many purposes
- baskets for berry picking and food storage
- cedar burial boxes
- woven clothing and waterproof rain hats
- feast dishes
- totem poles and sculptures

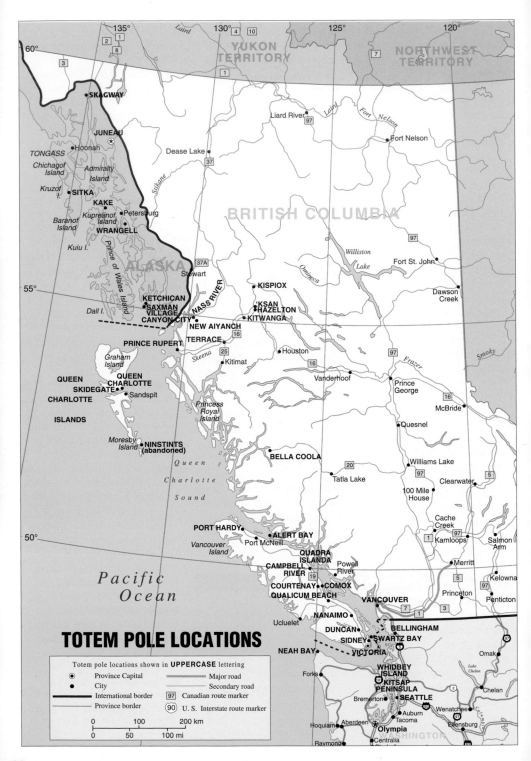

TOTEM POLE LOCATIONS

Totem pole locations shown in **UPPERCASE** lettering

⊙ Province Capital		Major road
• City		Secondary road
▬ International border	97	Canadian route marker
▬ Province border	90	U.S. Interstate route marker

0	100	200 km
0	50	100 mi

4. Land of the Totem Poles

Ever watchful eye

This chapter locates authentic, well-designed totem poles and totem pole collections from Seattle, Washington northward along the Pacific coast of British Columbia to Juneau, Alaska. Some of these totem poles have official names and some do not. The names listed here are descriptive only.

Alert Bay: Vancouver Island
Alert Bay is famous as the Kwakwaka'wakw village that defiantly continued its practice of the pot-latch at a time when it was illegal to do so.
• Collection of Poles—Restricted Namgis Cemetery
• World's Tallest Totem—Near U'mista Cultural Centre

Bella Coola
Bella Coola is an isolated village accessible along a difficult gravel road or by water. While there, it is advisable to request that an escort accompany you to view an area of rare petroglyphs.
• Small Collection and old Longhouse—Village centre

Bellingham: Washington
• Outdoor poles—Whatcom Museum of History and Art

Campbell River and Quadra Island: Vancouver Island
In and around Campbell River is the heart of Kwakiutl country—famous for the immortal Thunder-bird topping almost every pole. Quadra Island is a ten minute ferry ride from Campbell River.
• Big Man with Copper Pole—1400 We-Wai-Kum Road

- Cemetery Poles—Reserve, Band Cemetery
- Dzunkwa Pole—Tyee Plaza Shopping Centre lot
- House posts, Thunderbirds—Foreshore Park
- Kaysoo Crest Pole—Kwagiulth Museum, Quadra
- Two Poles—Coast Discovery Inn
- Thunderbird Pole—New Campbell River Museum
- Welcome Figure—Kwagiulth Museum, Quadra

Duncan: Vancouver Island

A walking tour map is available from the Cowichan Valley Museum on Canada Avenue and Station Street, Duncan, BC. Painted yellow footsteps lead the way to all 39 totem poles.

- Collection of Totems—Museum, Canada Ave & Station
- Collection of Totems—Walking Tour of Duncan
- Native Heritage Centre—Near Duncan Bridge
- Rick Hansen Memorial Pole—Museum grounds, Canada Ave
- World's Thickest Totem—Station Street and Jubilee

Haida Gwaii (the Queen Charlotte Islands)

The totem poles at Ninstints and Tanu are only accessible by boat or sea-plane. Tourists must leave each of these areas by nightfall. The Queen Charlotte Islands require a seven hour ferry crossing from Prince Rupert.

- Bill Reid Pole—Skidegate Band Office
- Davidson Poles—Old Masset
- Decaying Poles 1—Ninstints (by water)
- Decaying Poles 2—Tanu (by water)

In June of 1791 at Ninstints on Anthony Island, near the southern tip of the Haida Gwaii (Queen Charlotte Islands) a notorious atrocity occurred. American sea captain John Kendrick suffered the loss of his personal laundry from aboard his ship and responded (as was the naval custom of the day) by seizing a Haida chief and his companion. He ordered his crew to bolt their legs in a gun carriage, until the pilfered laundry was returned. To the proud chief Hoya, this was a grave insult.

Revenge was planned. When Kendrick and his men came ashore two weeks later, Hoya and his people swarmed aboard and commandeered his ship. Kendrick stalled, then delivered a counterattack killing more than 50 Haida people. Hoya himself was wounded.

Strong-arm tactics such as these, were not forgotten. As late as 1878, a Haida shaman's party, encountering Canadian researcher George Dawson, demanded to know if he was a "Boston" man. On being reassured by numerous references to British royalty, they left the research party alone.

Today, Ninstints, more properly called the village of Skungwaii, is an abandoned village in ruins. The remains of decaying totems loom in the frequents mists. Longhouses, shell middens, and more than two dozen totem poles, some at various angles, speak of a people who departed long ago. Abandoned since the smallpox epidemic of 1861, the site is teeming with nearby colonies of puffins, petrels, seals, and seabirds. Accessible only by water, many tour companies offer day trips into the area. The heritage site is under the administration of the Haida Gwaii Watchmen, a traditional society who have protected their island home for thousands of years.

Juneau, Alaska

Juneau, the gateway to Glacier Bay, has several totem poles and shelters a large brown bear and bald eagle population in the area.
- Centennial Poles—Centennial Hall, Egan Drive
- Century-old Totem—State Office Building
- Collection of Old Totems—Alaska State Museum
- Famous Lincoln Pole—Juneau Museum
- Two Poles—Auk Tribe Building

Kake, Alaska

The third tallest totem at 150 feet high is located here along with a collection of other totem poles.
- World's 3rd Tallest Totem—Kake

Ketchican, Alaska

According the U.S. National Record, Ketchican boasts the world's largest collection of original, old totem poles.
- Collection of Poles—Saxman Native Village
- Collection of Poles—Totem Bight Historical Site
- Collection of Poles—Totem Heritage Center
- Old Poles—Tongass Historical Museum

Kitsap Peninsula, Washington
- Chief's memorial—Suquamish Museum

'Ksan and Native Villages: Northwest British Columbia

Within a 50 kilometer radius of the reconstructed traditional native village of 'Ksan near New Hazelton BC, stand several collections of totem poles within Gitksan native villages.
- Bighouses and Poles—'Ksan Indian Village
- Collection of Poles 1—Gitsegukla
- Collection of Poles 2—Gitwangak
- Collection of Poles and Fort—Kitwanga
- Collection of Poles 3—Kitwancool
- Collection of Poles 4—Hazelton
- Totem poles and Hatchery—Kispiox
- United Pole—Kispiox Band Office

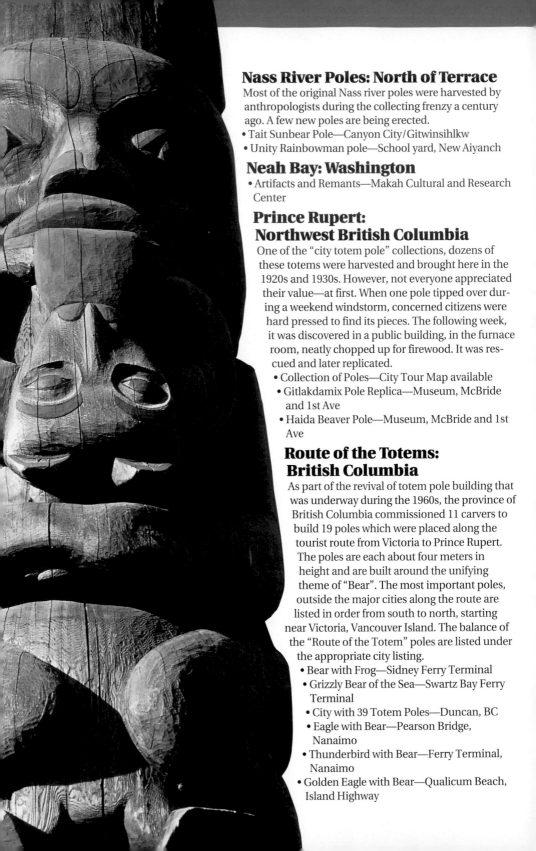

Nass River Poles: North of Terrace

Most of the original Nass river poles were harvested by anthropologists during the collecting frenzy a century ago. A few new poles are being erected.
• Tait Sunbear Pole—Canyon City/Gitwinsihlkw
• Unity Rainbowman pole—School yard, New Aiyanch

Neah Bay: Washington

• Artifacts and Remants—Makah Cultural and Research Center

Prince Rupert: Northwest British Columbia

One of the "city totem pole" collections, dozens of these totems were harvested and brought here in the 1920s and 1930s. However, not everyone appreciated their value—at first. When one pole tipped over during a weekend windstorm, concerned citizens were hard pressed to find its pieces. The following week, it was discovered in a public building, in the furnace room, neatly chopped up for firewood. It was rescued and later replicated.
• Collection of Poles—City Tour Map available
• Gitlakdamix Pole Replica—Museum, McBride and 1st Ave
• Haida Beaver Pole—Museum, McBride and 1st Ave

Route of the Totems: British Columbia

As part of the revival of totem pole building that was underway during the 1960s, the province of British Columbia commissioned 11 carvers to build 19 poles which were placed along the tourist route from Victoria to Prince Rupert. The poles are each about four meters in height and are built around the unifying theme of "Bear". The most important poles, outside the major cities along the route are listed in order from south to north, starting near Victoria, Vancouver Island. The balance of the "Route of the Totem" poles are listed under the appropriate city listing.
• Bear with Frog—Sidney Ferry Terminal
• Grizzly Bear of the Sea—Swartz Bay Ferry Terminal
• City with 39 Totem Poles—Duncan, BC
• Eagle with Bear—Pearson Bridge, Nanaimo
• Thunderbird with Bear—Ferry Terminal, Nanaimo
• Golden Eagle with Bear—Qualicum Beach, Island Highway

- Kolus Pole—Infocentre, Courtenay
- Twin Poles—Lewis Park, Courtenay
- Hok Hok with Sun and Chief—Comox Reserve, Bighouse
- Grizzly Bear with Salmon—Port Hardy Ferry Terminal

Seattle, Washington
In addition to the Goodwill Pole at Pioneer Square, there are a number of well carved poles scattered around Seattle.
- Artifacts and Poles—Thomas Burke Memorial Washington State Museum, U of Washington
- Chief John Wallace's Pole—MonHake Cut on E.Shelby Street
- Duane Pasco Collection—Occidental Square
- Goodwill Pole and others—Pioneer Square
- Poles and Feasting—Blake Island
- Seattle Center Pole—Corner of Center House
- Traditional Poles—North of Pike Place Market

Sitka, Alaska
With prevalent reminders of its Russian occupation, Sitka also features authentic totem poles and a cultural center. Some of the oldest intact poles in the world are found here.
- Collection of 28 totem poles—Sitka National Historical Park

Terrace and Kitsumkulum, Northwest British Columbia
The native community of Kitsumkulum is only a few kilometers from Terrace. Since most of the original poles in the area were harvested in the great museum collecting frenzy about 100 years ago, these are poles are about a decade old.
- Diamond Jubilee Pole—3205 Eby Street
- Two Poles—Highway 16 near Terrace

Vancouver and Area: Lower Mainland
One of the finest totem collections in the world is found at the Museum of Anthropology, 6393 NW Marine Drive. There is also a small simulated native village outdoors on the grounds.
- Bear Mother Poles—VanDusen Gardens, 37th & Oak
- Centennial 100' Pole—Maritime Museum, Cypress St.

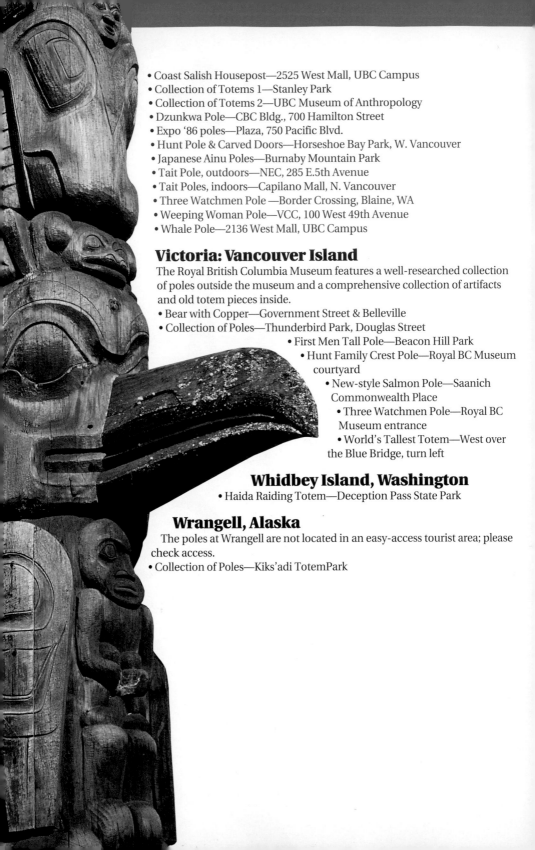

- Coast Salish Housepost—2525 West Mall, UBC Campus
- Collection of Totems 1—Stanley Park
- Collection of Totems 2—UBC Museum of Anthropology
- Dzunkwa Pole—CBC Bldg., 700 Hamilton Street
- Expo '86 poles—Plaza, 750 Pacific Blvd.
- Hunt Pole & Carved Doors—Horseshoe Bay Park, W. Vancouver
- Japanese Ainu Poles—Burnaby Mountain Park
- Tait Pole, outdoors—NEC, 285 E.5th Avenue
- Tait Poles, indoors—Capilano Mall, N. Vancouver
- Three Watchmen Pole —Border Crossing, Blaine, WA
- Weeping Woman Pole—VCC, 100 West 49th Avenue
- Whale Pole—2136 West Mall, UBC Campus

Victoria: Vancouver Island

The Royal British Columbia Museum features a well-researched collection of poles outside the museum and a comprehensive collection of artifacts and old totem pieces inside.

- Bear with Copper—Government Street & Belleville
- Collection of Poles—Thunderbird Park, Douglas Street
- First Men Tall Pole—Beacon Hill Park
- Hunt Family Crest Pole—Royal BC Museum courtyard
- New-style Salmon Pole—Saanich Commonwealth Place
- Three Watchmen Pole—Royal BC Museum entrance
- World's Tallest Totem—West over the Blue Bridge, turn left

Whidbey Island, Washington

- Haida Raiding Totem—Deception Pass State Park

Wrangell, Alaska

The poles at Wrangell are not located in an easy-access tourist area; please check access.

- Collection of Poles—Kiks'adi TotemPark

Reference

Recommended Reading

Barbeau, Marius. *Totem Poles.* Ottawa: Queens Printer, 1950.

Brown, Jospeh Epes. *The Spiritual Legacy of the American Indian.* New York: Crossroad Publishing Company, 1982

Drew, Leslie & Douglas Wilson. *Argillite, Art of the Haida.* Surrey, BC: Hancock House, 1980.

Efrat, Barbara S. and W.J. Langois. *Captain Cook and the Spanish Explorers on the Coast.* Victoria, B.C.: Sound Heritage, Queens Printer, 1978.

——. *The History and Survival of Nootkan Culture.* Victoria, B.C.: Sound Heritage, Queens Printer, 1978.

Feest, Christian. *Native Arts of North America.* London: Thames and Hudson, 1992.

Gill, Sam D. & Irene F. Sullivan. *Dictionary of Native American Mythology.* New York: Oxford University Press, 1992.

Goodchild, Peter. *Raven Tales: Traditional Stories of Native Peoples.* Chicago: Chicago Review Press, 1991.

Gunther, Erna. *Art in the Life of Northwest Coast Indians.* Portland: Portland Art Museum, 1966.

Hawthorne, Audrey. *Kwakiutl Art.* Seattle: University of Washington Press; Vancouver: Douglas & McIntrye, 1988.

Holm, Bill. *Northwest Coast Indian Art: An Analysis of Form.* Seattle: University of Washington Press; Vancouver: Douglas & McIntrye, 1965.

——, *Spirit and Ancestor.* Douglas and McIntyre, Vancouver, 1987.

Jonaitis, Aldona, ed. *Chiefly Feasts, the Enduring Kwakiutl Potlatch.* Seattle: University of Washington Press; Vancouver: Douglas & McIntyre, 1991.

——. *Art of the Northern Tlingit.* Seattle: University of Washington Press, 1986.

Kew, Della, and P.E. Goddard. *Indian Art and Culture.* Vancouver: Hancock House, 1974.

MacDonald, George F. and John J. Cove. *Tsimshian Narratives 1.* Collected by Marius Barbeau and William Beynon, Canadian Museum of Civilization, Mercury Series. Ottawa, 1987.

——. *Tsimshian Narratives 2.* Collected by Marius Barbeau and William Beynon, Canadian Museum of Civilization, Mercury Series. Ottawa, 1987.

Macnair, Peter L. *The Legacy.* Vancouver: Douglas and McIntyre, 1984.

Maud, Ralph. *A Guide to B.C. Indian Myth and Legend.* Vancouver: Talonbooks, 1982.

Nuytten, Phil. *The Totem Carvers: Charlie James, Ellen Neel and Mungo Martin.* Panorama Publications, 1982.

Sommer, Robin Langley. *Native American Art.* London: Bison Group, 1994.

Stewart, Hilary. *Looking at Indian Art of the Northwest Coast.* Vancouver: Douglas and McIntyre, 1979.

——. *Looking at Totem Poles.* Vancouver: Douglas and McIntyre, 1993.

University of British Columbia. Museum of Anthropology. *Northwest Coast Indian Artifacts.* Vancouver: University of British Columbia, 1975.

Wallas, James, and Pamela Whitaker. *Kwakiutl Legends.* Surrey, BC: Hancock House, 1989.

Wardell, Allen. *Objects of Bright Pride,* 1978.

Index

Photographic Credits

All photographs including back cover are by the author except as noted below:
B.C. Archives and Records Service: 11 (b-03660), 14 (h-03990), 19 left (d-00252), 20 top (h-04231), 22 top (b-03593), 25 top (g-05055), 26 right (h-04132), 34 left (h-04137), 34 right (e-07361), 36 (e-06968), 50 top (f-04182), 55 (h-03982)

Jo Curran, Rainbow Horizon Tours: 75, 78 top, 82

Royal British Columbia Museum: 46 (PN 100 72)
New Zealand Tourist Authority: 22

Ricardo Ordóñez: front cover

The Author

A long-time resident of British Columbia's West Coast, Pat Kramer is a naturalist and speaker who works on cruise ships. She has travelled the world, visiting First Peoples, and is an acknowledged expert on the cultures of Northwest Coast First Nations, with whom she worked in educational capacities for more than 20 years.

An accomplished writer and photographer, she has written several special-interest books, including *British Columbia For Free: And Almost Free, Gardens of British Columbia, Native Sites in Western Canada* and *Alaska's Totem Poles.*

Pat Kramer